THE COMPLETE GUIDE TO
TAROT AND ASTROLOGY

THE COMPLETE GUIDE
TO TAROT AND
ASTROLOGY

EVERYTHING YOU NEED TO KNOW TO HARNESS THE WISDOM OF THE CARDS AND THE STARS

LOUISE EDINGTON

ROCKRIDGE
PRESS

I dedicate this book to my husband and life partner, Charles, who tolerates my witchy ways. I love you to the moon and back.

CONTENTS

INTRODUCTION

WELCOME TO THIS COMPREHENSIVE GUIDE to using astrology to enhance, deepen, and expand tarot readings for growth and self-discovery through an understanding of astrology within tarot.

I am Louise Edington, author of two books, *Modern Astrology* and *The Complete Guide to Astrology*, both of which were written to create deeper understanding of the self and to support personal growth. Although I'm primarily an astrologer, I have long integrated the Tarot into my work, as the two are aligned, and each deepens the understanding of the other. Both tools aid with arriving at a deep self-acceptance and understanding of our own inner workings, and both help us tune in to our intuition and inner voice so that we can grow and live in love and alignment with the energies of the universe.

Both astrology and tarot found me in 1989, as I went through my first Saturn return at the age of 29, a time of major maturation, when Saturn returns to the place it was during our time of birth. I still have my first deck, a **Rider-Waite Tarot Deck**, but in recent years I have come to use the **Thoth Deck** more consistently. I use each tool to enhance the practice of the other, and after over 30 years with both, the elements and the planetary energies have deepened my understanding of each card.

Both astrology and tarot are symbolic maps of our consciousness. Tarot is more accessible than astrology in that it's a more intuitive form of divination, whereas astrology requires study. Using the two in tandem creates a deeper understanding and alignment with our innermost voice as reflected by the hermetic axiom: "That which is above is like to that which is below, and that which is below is like to that which is above." In other words, working with both tools together can give us a road map for living a life that is aligned with our highest selves and the whole of the universe.

This book is for both beginners and those who want to understand how to integrate astrology into their advanced tarot practice. It will help you read the Tarot at a very deep level and open new ways of exploring the Tarot for personal growth.

The book begins with an introduction to tarot, astrology, and the foundational knowledge you'll need to approach these practices with confidence. The book then walks you through how to read the cards using astrology, interpret spreads, and build your knowledge of each card.

This book will give you an effective way to work through complicated feelings and questions that can come up during periods of intense personal growth. However, any mental health concerns should be addressed by a medical professional. Neither tarot nor astrology is a replacement for medical treatment or therapy, and there is no shame in seeking help.

Incorporating astrology and tarot into your life opens your eyes to a whole new way of learning about yourself and how the world around you works. My own life and work is a testament to that, as are the lives of hundreds of clients. Using the Tarot with an understanding of astrology will lead you to the innermost truths of your higher self. Enjoy!

I

THE **FOUNDATIONS** OF TAROT & ASTROLOGY

Part I will cover a brief introduction to tarot, astrology, their essential elements, and how they can be used together for self-reflection, self-discovery, and personal growth. Part I takes you through the basics of the history, origins, key figures, and evolution of the Tarot, the Major and Minor Arcana, the individual cards, the suits, planets, houses, and modalities, as well as how astrology and tarot work together, before offering guidance for reading your cards through the lens of astrology and sample spreads and readings.

1

TAROT 101

In this chapter, you will learn the very basics of tarot, and the essential elements. This includes how to work with the Tarot; a brief overview of the ritual, origins, history, and key figures associated with the Tarot; and how tarot has evolved and other spiritual practices connected to the Tarot. There is also a brief overview of the 78 tarot cards in the deck. Part II will demonstrate how astrology can enhance your understanding of the cards. However, it's important that you first understand the basics.

THE RITUAL OF TAROT

Ritual has been an important part of human lives for millennia. Through ritual, we celebrate significant times in our lives and the world. Birth, death, the turning of the seasons, and more are all celebrated by various rituals throughout the world. Most of us have daily rituals, such as our morning cup of coffee, a daily walk, meditation, or journaling.

Rituals both mark and create time, and structure our worlds, fostering a sense of belonging and shared experiences.

The Tarot is a ritual, a time to stop and reflect, to mark time and tune in to a deeper place and to receive guidance, whether it's regarding specific questions or just life in general. The ritual allows you to find your innermost voice reflected in the cards. The ritual of a card for the day sets the tone and suggests how to move throughout your day, for example, whether it be a caution regarding internal blocks and distractions or inspiration. A larger spread, which we'll look at in this book, provides guidance for navigating greater questions.

TAROT CAN HELP YOU DIG DEEPER

The tarot cards contain imagery, symbolism, and stories that unlock our inner wisdom and subconscious self to reveal the journey and story of our lives. Tarot is used to receive guidance by tuning in to the intuitive higher self and to archetypal imagery and symbolism that can help us understand the soul's journey and receive answers to pressing questions. It's believed that tarot contains a blueprint to consciousness that can help us tune in to both spiritual and practical guidance throughout our lives.

In other words, the Tarot helps reveal our inner wisdom, and we "read" that wisdom through the symbolism of the cards. The cards illuminate possibilities and choices, aiding us in making decisions to open the next path for us. By tuning in to a tarot reading, whether it be a single card or a spread, you are making the space to reflect on your innermost thoughts as they are projected onto the cards.

Make Time for Self-Reflection & Self-Discovery

Many people do not make time for self-reflection and self-discovery among the busyness of life. Making this time enables you to pause and sort through tangled experiences and observations so that you can process where you are coming from and where you are going. This helps reduce overwhelming feelings, facilitates breakthroughs in your personal growth, and increases self-love and acceptance, allowing you to live life more intentionally, rather than just meandering through life from a less-conscious perspective.

Commit to Personal Growth

I invite you to commit to your personal growth by using the tools of tarot and astrology to reflect on who you are and the potential you have within by making the space for deep reflection on your habits, skills, and gifts so that you can strive to be your higher self at all times.

This requires a desire to learn and grow, a willingness to make changes, and an open mind. It's a rewarding journey leading to more fulfilling relationships in all areas of your life but, most important, to a more rewarding relationship with yourself. Through a commitment to personal growth, you can learn to love yourself more while developing into a more loving, compassionate, and optimistic person.

Discover a Form of Divination

The word **divination** comes from the Latin word *divinus*, meaning to be inspired by the divine. Divination itself is the practice of gaining insight into questions and situations through the ritual use of specific tools. Divination is not, despite what some may say, fortune-telling. As discussed earlier, the Tarot and other divination tools are used to gain insight into our own inner voice, intuition, and higher self.

There are many forms of divination, including those that use pendulums, tea leaves, and the *I Ching*, a classic ancient Chinese book of divination. Tarot, however, offers so much more, as the symbolism and imagery connect us to many other divinatory systems, including astrology, one of the most ancient accounts of the stars.

THE EVOLUTION OF THE TAROT DECK

The origins of tarot are shrouded in mystery, with no clear evolution. There's a lot of evidence that the tarot deck developed from 52 playing cards that came to Europe from China and from the Islamic world via the Silk Road in the late 14th century. Islamic playing cards called Mamluk cards had four suits plus three court cards. These are like the playing cards used in many card games today.

The Tarot itself is thought to have developed in Italy in the early 15th century, when extra cards, now known as the 22-card Major Arcana, were added by Bonifacio Bembo for the Visconti family in Milan. "Arcana" means secret or mysteries. These were added to the 56-playing-card deck that was divided into four suits, of which the Minor Arcana still consists.

The Tarot was originally a gaming deck known as *carte da trionfi*, or triumph cards, with the additional cards known simply as trionfi, which became "trumps" in English. Known by various names, the Tarot as a gaming deck is still used as playing cards in various places in mainland Europe.

Europeans modified the suits from scimitars, polo sticks, cups, and coins to swords, batons, cups, and coins, whereas the court cards changed to depict human figures.

By the late 15th century, the tarot deck had evolved into the 78-card structure we generally use today: 22 trump cards, now known as the Major Arcana, and 4 suits with 14 cards, each including 4 court cards.

The Tarot de Marseille Deck created by Parisian Jean Noblet in 1650 is one of the earliest decks that is still used today, thanks to restoration by Jean-Claude Flornoy. This deck forms the basis of the imagery on the Rider-Waite-Smith Deck, though the Minor Arcana especially was simpler and more like playing card decks. From this point on, various decks were developed using Egyptian and Qabalistic symbolism, such as the Tree of Life.

Although the Tarot was initially developed as a playing card deck, signs of the divinatory use of the cards began to emerge with the discovery of a 1740 manuscript. This gave divinatory meaning to a 35-card deck, the Tarocco Bolognese.

The Tarot was not used widely as a divinatory oracle, or cartomancy, until the late 18th century, though some tarot enthusiasts claim links to other ancient divinatory and symbolic systems, including from ancient Egyptian times. There is no scholarly historical evidence of this other than the symbolism used in some decks. The Thoth Deck in particular uses symbols from many ancient traditions.

When tarot reached the English-speaking West in the late 19th century, and with the founding of the Hermetic Order of the Golden Dawn (a secret society devoted to the study and practice of the occult, metaphysics, and the paranormal during the late 19th and early 20th centuries) in 1886, tarot as we now know it really began to grow.

There are a few key figures in the evolution of the Tarot. Etteilla, a pseudonym for Jean-Baptiste Alliette, was the first-known professional tarot reader. His 1783 book, *How to Entertain Oneself with a Pack of Cards Called Tarot*, contained the first guide to using the Tarot for divination. Etteilla also created the first tarot deck using hermetic teachings in the illustrations.

Two of the most influential figures in tarot are A. E. Waite, who published the Rider-Waite-Smith Deck, and Aleister Crowley, who published the Thoth Deck. Both came from the Hermetic Order of the Golden Dawn. Let's take a closer look at these two decks.

Rider-Waite-Smith Deck

The Rider-Waite-Smith Deck is the most well-known, influential, and commonly used tarot deck. It is more formally known as the Rider-Waite Deck, after the creator and the publisher, omitting the name of the artist, Pamela Colman Smith. The artist's name has been included in more recent years, and her contribution acknowledged. This deck became the most widely used tarot, especially after 1959, when the deck was published by University Books and, later, U.S. Games, Inc., primarily because of the selling power behind a major publisher. The text of this book is primarily based on that deck.

Created in 1909, much of the symbolism in the deck is from Christian and Judaic mysticism and astrological attributions, and is influenced heavily by the work of Etteilla and both Waite and Smith's membership in the Hermetic Order of the Golden Dawn, which studied the occult and challenged conventional religions. Unlike some decks, the Rider-Waite-Smith Deck is less overtly occult.

Crowley-Thoth Deck

Arguably the second most influential deck was created by another former member of the Hermetic Order of the Golden Dawn, Aleister Crowley.

From around 1938 to 1942, Frieda Harris, Crowley's student, created the original artwork for Crowley's Thoth Deck, based on his channeled text, *The Book of Law*, of which the central message was: "Do what thou wilt shall be the whole of the law; love is the law, love under will." This message is reflected in the complex imagery of personal transformation and growth contained in the Thoth Deck.

The original paintings for the Thoth Deck were created and exhibited in 1942 by artist Frieda Harris in a gallery in London. A limited edition of the deck was published in 1944. The deck wasn't published after that limited edition until 1969. It is more esoteric in nature than the Rider-Waite-Smith Deck, drawing on symbols from the Qabalah, astrology, alchemy (the transformation of matter), and numerology (the study of numbers), among other references.

Tarot Today

The Tarot has continued to evolve since its conception. Today, you can find thousands of different decks. Similarly, there are thousands of websites teaching the meaning of the Tarot, from individual cards to spreads to teachings about the soul's journey through the Tarot.

The intention of this book is to open possibilities for you, as the Tarot is a deeply intuitive form of divination and the symbols on the cards vary from deck to deck. There are core meanings commonly used in decks, but the connection to the cards is very intuitive, and I invite you to develop what you learn in this book through practice, no matter what deck you use.

Modern & Inclusive Imagery

Many modern tarot decks have evolved to integrate more inclusive imagery that reflects the diversity of our human experience, with figures of all colors, sizes, and orientations, moving away from the Eurocentric, white, binary, and patriarchal origins of the Tarot. The accompanying deck to this book is designed to use such inclusive imagery. This evolution is also occurring in the world of astrology, where there are major efforts to use more inclusive language and imagery as well.

The intention in this section is to open up possibilities for you, as the Tarot is a deeply intuitive form of divination, and the symbols on the cards vary from deck to deck. There are core meanings commonly used in decks, but the connection to the cards is very intuitive and I invite you to take what you learn in this book and allow it to develop through practice.

COMMON MISCONCEPTIONS OF TAROT

One of the primary misconceptions is that the Tarot predicts the future. Whether this is true really depends on your beliefs. Readers have predicted outcomes with varying degrees of accuracy. Personally, I believe human beings have free will and no outcome is fixed. Tarot is more useful as a tool for deep understanding and personal growth.

Another misconception is that your first deck needs to be gifted, but you *can* buy your own deck. The power is not in the deck but in the intuitive understanding.

Yet another misconception is the fear that the Tarot is magic and dangerous, with good and bad cards. None of this is true. The cards are a self-reflective tool, and all cards have multiple meanings depending on their placement on a spread or the needs of the subject.

AN OVERVIEW OF THE 78 CARDS

In this section, we'll look at an overview of all 78 cards of the Tarot before an overview of astrology, and then we will dive deeper into using astrology to add to your understanding of the Tarot.

The Tarot uses symbolism from various traditions, archetypes, elements (i.e., earth, air, fire, and water), and stories to guide us through making choices, personal development, manifesting goals, and more. It's a tool to access inner wisdom—a soul mirror.

The 22 **Major Arcana** cards represent spiritual lessons and a journey to individuation and spiritual enlightenment. The cards offer an exploration through archetypal stories and are primarily based on the Fool's (the innocent) journey and personal growth from innocence to enlightenment.

The 56 **Minor Arcana** cards represent more worldly, daily situations and activities, and are organized into four suits corresponding to the elements earth, air, fire, and water.

The 16 **court cards** represent personality characteristics, or archetypes, which we may express at different times and, often, other people in our lives. These cards are based on different figures in a royal court: the Page, Knight, Queen, and King, as this imagery is well understood in a hierarchical society and represents people who influence a situation in a reading. That can include the **querent** themselves (the person who is seeking wisdom or a reading). Each card also has astrological correspondences.

An understanding of and attunement to the different symbolism and imagery and how they work together leads to real magic in tarot readings.

The 22 Major Arcana Cards

The cards in the Major Arcana form the foundation of the deck, and the archetypal significance is most pronounced in these cards. The 22 cards take us through the innocent wonder of the Fool's journey—a metaphor for the journey through life, of spiritual enlightenment, and individuation—to the fullness of the World card.

The soul's journey through the Major Arcana is often divided into a spread with the Fool as the querent, or innocent, starting on a journey of personal growth, and the remaining 21 cards divided into three lines of seven, with each line representing consciousness (gaining awareness of your role in life), the subconscious (inner journey of individuation), and superconscious (the development of a spiritual awareness). I strongly suggest laying the cards out in this way while you study the Major Arcana. These cards also represent longer-term situations.

The 56 Minor Arcana Cards

The 56 Minor Arcana cards address more mundane matters and more immediate worldly situations and events, as well as energy moving through our lives in the moment. They give more of a guide as to what actions can be taken in your day-to-day life.

There are four different suits within the Minor Arcana.

The suit of cups is associated with the element of water and represents emotions, intuition, and creativity.

The suit of pentacles (or disks in some decks) is associated with the element of earth and represents material and physical matters.

The suit of swords is associated with air and represents the mind, communication, and decisions.

The suit of wands is associated with fire and represents life force, will, passion, and spirituality.

NUMBERS (ACE THROUGH 10)

Each suit in the Minor Arcana consists of 14 cards, ace to 10 plus the court cards. The symbolism of the numbers from 1 to 10 are the same for each suit.

Simply speaking, the significance of the numbers is as follows:

1. Beginnings
2. Balance
3. Creation
4. Foundation or Stability
5. Change
6. Harmony
7. Reflection
8. Mastery
9. Accomplishment
10. Completion

THE COURT CARDS (PAGE, KNIGHT, QUEEN & KING)

There are four court cards in each suit, and they represent personalities. Sometimes that might be the querent, a part of the self, or another person in the querent's life.

The King is the mature, active expression of the suit. The Queen is the mature, receptive expression. The Knight is the young, active expression. And the Page is the young, receptive expression.

CUPS (ACE THROUGH KING)

The cups suit is related to the element of water and the astrological Sun signs Cancer, Scorpio, and Pisces. The element of water represents emotion, love, creativity, intuition, compassion, healing, and imagination.

PENTACLES (ACE THROUGH KING)

Pentacles are related to the element of earth and the astrological Sun signs Taurus, Virgo, and Capricorn. They represent being grounded and are reflective of the material world and the concept of manifestation and of being firm, reliable, responsible, and steady. Because pentacles represent the material world, this also connects the cards to our resources, nature, the body, and financial matters.

SWORDS (ACE THROUGH KING)

The element of air and the astrological Sun signs Gemini, Libra, and Aquarius are the realm of the swords suit. This suit represents the realm of ideas, communication, curiosity, knowledge, and mental organization. Swords are sharp and cut cleanly. It's helpful to remember that words can be used to harm as well as to carry messages like the wind.

WANDS (ACE THROUGH KING)

The wands suit is the suit of fire and corresponds with the astrological Sun signs Aries, Leo, and Sagittarius. It cleanses and purifies and is connected to our life force and willpower. Fire is volatile, fast moving, and connected to inspiration, passion, and adventure. However, fire can burn things down, though that also means new creation from the ashes.

THERE IS A RANGE OF SPIRITUAL PRACTICES CONNECTED TO TAROT

The symbolism contained in the Tarot is connected to a whole realm of other spiritual practices. Some readers use **numerology** (the study of the meaning of numbers) in connection with the numbers of the cards, though others say the numbers work differently in the Tarot.

The Hebrew alphabet and the Qabalistic Tree of Life have 22 letters or paths, the same number of cards in the Major Arcana, and are said to contain the whole of existence, a complete inner road map. The Qabalah is also connected to the number 10 with the 10 Commandments and 10 stages of emanation (based on archetypal parts of the self), as well as to sephiroth, or the 10 powers by which the divine is said to become manifest. There are 10 numbered cards in each suit. There are other Qabalistic references in the Tarot, and the imagery, the alphabet, and the Tree of Life,

for example, certainly show up in some of the cards. However, the historical origins of any such connection are hazy.

Tarot has also been connected to witchcraft, and although many Wiccans use it for divination, the Tarot is a tool and Witchcraft, Paganism, and Wicca, are spiritual practices and lifestyles.

The symbolism of the Tarot relates to many other practices or tenets of spiritual practice, such as the seven-chakra system. (*Chakra*, or *cakra* in Sanskrit, means "wheel" and refers to energy points in your body.)

It's my view that we see reflected in the cards that which is meant for us as an intuitive tool of divination. The cards can lead us to deeper study of the symbolism, but knowledge of, for example, the Qabalah, isn't necessary to glean the message meant for you.

THE 22 MAJOR ARCANA CARDS

THE FOOL

THE MAGICIAN

THE HIGH PRIESTESS

THE EMPRESS

THE EMPEROR

THE HIEROPHANT

THE LOVERS

THE CHARIOT

STRENGTH

THE HERMIT

WHEEL OF FORTUNE

JUSTICE

THE HANGED MAN

DEATH

TEMPERANCE

THE DEVIL

THE TOWER

THE STAR

THE MOON

THE SUN

JUDGMENT

THE WORLD

Cups

ACE OF CUPS

2 OF CUPS

3 OF CUPS

4 OF CUPS

5 OF CUPS

6 OF CUPS

7 OF CUPS

8 OF CUPS

9 OF CUPS

10 OF CUPS

PAGE OF CUPS

KNIGHT OF CUPS

QUEEN OF CUPS

KING OF CUPS

ACE OF PENTACLES

2 OF PENTACLES

3 OF PENTACLES

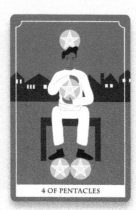

4 OF PENTACLES

5 OF PENTACLES

6 OF PENTACLES

7 OF PENTACLES

8 OF PENTACLES

9 OF PENTACLES

10 OF PENTACLES

PAGE OF PENTACLES

KNIGHT OF PENTACLES

QUEEN OF PENTACLES

KING OF PENTACLES

ACE OF SWORDS

2 OF SWORDS

3 OF SWORDS

4 OF SWORDS

5 OF SWORDS

THE COMPLETE GUIDE TO TAROT AND ASTROLOGY

6 OF SWORDS

7 OF SWORDS

8 OF SWORDS

9 OF SWORDS

10 OF SWORDS

PAGE OF SWORDS

KNIGHT OF SWORDS

QUEEN OF SWORDS

KING OF SWORDS

ACE OF WANDS

2 OF WANDS

3 OF WANDS

4 OF WANDS

5 OF WANDS

6 OF WANDS

7 OF WANDS

8 OF WANDS

9 OF WANDS

10 OF WANDS

PAGE OF WANDS

KNIGHT OF WANDS

QUEEN OF WANDS

KING OF WANDS

ASTROLOGY CAN PLAY A MAJOR ROLE IN YOUR READING OF THE CARDS

Basic knowledge of astrology can really help you read the cards at a deep level. Both astrology and the Tarot are connected to the elements, but the connections run deeper than that.

Astrology is the practice of interpreting the planets, which represent parts of the self or the "what" in the 12 signs, how the planets work in those signs, and the areas of life they are working in at any given moment—the "where" or the houses. There are other astrological factors, such as modalities and decans, and all of these can be found

represented in the Tarot, as I will show you in the next chapters.

By combining an understanding of the planetary energies, the signs, and more with the symbolism in the cards, we reach a greater depth of insight in Tarot readings. I want to emphasize that this takes practice and time. I find that new understandings reveal themselves even after years of practice. Have patience with yourself and trust that the insights you receive are perfect for any moment.

LET'S GET STARTED

In this chapter, we've looked at the very basics of the Tarot, a brief history, some of the key figures, and the anatomy of a Tarot deck.

Take some time to reflect on the information with your tarot deck. Tuning in to the actual cards is far more important than developing a rational understanding, as there is no one way to understand a card. As you will see moving through the rest of the book, it's a matter of building an in-depth intuitive understanding rather than learning by rote memorization.

I suggest reading each section and then sitting with your cards and meditating on what you have learned as you go through the deck. Journaling your insights can also help. Do this at every step of the way.

Next, we will look at the basics of astrology and then move on to integrate your tarot practice with astrology. We'll also look more at how the integration of this, and an understanding of other spiritual practices, can enhance your understanding.

2

ASTROLOGY 101

In this chapter, you will learn the very basics of astrology—the modalities, elements, planets and luminaries, houses, and signs. We'll also take a brief look at the very extensive history of and major figures in astrology. Astrology is so much more than the 12 Sun signs and has evolved to become a powerful tool for personal growth and self-acceptance. You will learn how astrology has evolved and how it is used in modern times. An understanding of these basics will bring added depth to your tarot practice.

WHAT IS ASTROLOGY?

Astrology is the study of the movement and cycles of the planetary bodies in the solar system and how those influences work in human lives and in our natural world.

There are many uses for astrology, including psychological, mundane (world events), medical, electional (picking fortuitous dates and times), horary (answering a specific question), predictive, relationship, and **natal** (based on date, time, and location of birth). There are also different traditions, such as Western and Jyotish (Vedic). The basics, however, permeate all types, and so this book will focus on those basics.

My personal approach and that of this book and my two previous books, *The Complete Guide to Astrology* and *Modern Astrology*, is that of personal growth and the soul's evolution and potential—a more psychological approach. Using astrology to deepen your tarot practice, however, brings in elements of all types of astrology. By understanding that the planetary energies influence human beings and how people respond to those energies, you can begin to see how astrology can also deepen your understanding of the Tarot.

THE ORIGINS OF ASTROLOGY

Astrology has existed in some form since humans were cave dwellers, as there is evidence that lunar cycles were tracked on bones and in cave paintings.

From the fifth to third millennia BCE, the Sumerians in Mesopotamia identified and followed the movements of the visible planets. Vedic astrology (a traditional Hindu system) is thought to be at least 5,000 years old, with some estimates that the practice may have been practiced as early as 10,000 BCE in the region now known as India.

The Babylonians, later known as the Chaldeans, laid the foundations of what would become Western astrology with the creation of the zodiac wheel, the degree system, and the concept of 12 houses. This period was from around 2400 to 331 BCE. The Chaldean priest astronomers of the late Babylonian period developed models to predict the planetary movements and even suggested that the Sun was the center of the system and that the Moon affected the tides.

The planets and zodiac signs were given their modern names by the Greeks. In 140 CE, Claudius Ptolemy, a Greek mathematician, astronomer, philosopher, and astrologer, published *Tetrabiblos*, a series of four books that contained the names of the planets, houses, aspects, and angles, all of which are used by astrologers today.

Key History

In the West, the popularity and use of astrology has waxed and waned over time. In the Middle Ages, it was learned alongside mathematics, astronomy, and medicine. In fact, the oldest universities had astrology chairs, and there were royal astrologers.

Astrology then declined during the Age of Reason in the 17th and 18th centuries, when it was sidelined as an entertainment. It didn't regain popularity again in the West until the 19th century and onward, when the development of psychoanalysis coincided with a renewed interest in spirituality.

Key Figures

In the 17th century, Placidus de Titus, the Italian monk and professor of mathematics, expanded on the astrological practice of the Greeks by introducing a house system, which is commonly used today. Later in the century, William Lilly, an English astrologer, published the first English-language astrology text in 1647.

During its revival in the late 19th century, astrological practices continued to evolve under the influence of people like Alan Leo, a British author who focused on interpreting characters rather than events. Carl Jung, a Swiss psychiatrist and psychoanalyst, was one of the leading influences in psychology but also studied astrology and wrote that "astrology represents the sum of all the psychological knowledge of antiquity." Dane Rudhyar became known as a pioneer of modern humanistic astrology.

ASTROLOGY IN MODERN TIMES

Astrology today seems to be having a resurgence. Astrologers such as Chris Brennan, who wrote *Hellenistic Astrology: The Study of Fate and Fortune*, are investigating and rediscovering ancient astrological techniques and texts and reintroducing some of those techniques. Astrologer Demetra George has also reintroduced a lot of traditional techniques through her book *Ancient Astrology in Theory and Practice: A Manual of Traditional Techniques.* And Robert Hand, an American astrologer, historian, author, and scholar, has also contributed to the revival and translation of historical astrological texts.

In today's modern practice of astrology, it's common to see a greater integration of other techniques, such as shamanic or religious practices connected to the spirit world, counseling and self-care practices, psychosynthesis and therapeutic approaches that focus on self-growth and development, and, of course, tarot.

Today, social media has introduced people to "pop astrology" and memes. Astrological phenomena such as zodiac (Sun) signs and Mercury retrograde (when Mercury appears to go backward through the zodiac from our perspective) have achieved common use in the English language. This can lead us to a deeper study of astrology but can also lead to some misunderstandings about meanings.

ASTROLOGY GOES BEYOND THE 12 STAR (SUN) SIGNS

Astrology is so much more than the 12 **Sun signs** (so-called because of the position of the Sun at a person's birth). Astrology consists of all the planetary bodies, signs, elements, modalities, angles, aspects, and more. The Sun signs are merely easiest to know by date alone.

An astrological horoscope is created by a calculation using the date, time, and place of birth or of an event. Luckily for us, there are free online tools that calculate horoscopes (see the resources section at the end of this book for some suggestions).

The following sections contain a brief description of the modalities, elements, planets and luminaries, houses, and Sun signs. In subsequent chapters, you'll learn about the astrological correspondences with the Tarot. I want to emphasize that practice is the only way to fully integrate the knowledge in this book. Practicing readings, meditating or journaling on the cards, and rereading the sections as you practice will help you absorb the information over time and integrate your own intuitive understanding.

Planetary cycles, or orbital periods, is an aspect of astrology that can help deepen your astrological tarot practice. For example, Saturn takes between 28 and 30 years to orbit around the Sun. Approximately every seven years, Saturn revisits the place it was at in a horoscope, indicating a period of major growth. Awareness of those time periods can further deepen your work with the Tarot.

The orbital periods are as follows:

PLANETARY BODY	ORBITAL PERIOD
MOON	29.5 days to complete one orbit of the Earth
MERCURY	88 days to complete one orbit of the Sun
VENUS	224.5 days to complete one orbit of the Sun
SUN	1 year to complete the cycle of the zodiac
MARS	22 months to complete one orbit of the Sun
JUPITER	12 years to complete one orbit of the Sun
SATURN	28 to 30 years to complete one orbit of the Sun
URANUS	84 years to complete one orbit of the Sun
NEPTUNE	165 years to complete one orbit of the Sun
PLUTO	248 years (approximately) to complete one orbit of the Sun

THE THREE MODALITIES

Astrology divides the 12 astrological signs into three modalities, meaning how the signs operate or express differently. In other words, it's the mode of operation, temperament, or attitude of each of the signs. The three modalities are cardinal, fixed, and mutable.

The modalities are also known as quadruplicities, as there are four astrological signs in each modality. The three modalities repeat in the same order around the zodiac: cardinal, fixed, and mutable. Each person will have all modalities represented within their horoscope but will usually have one that dominates with more planetary bodies. This dominant modality will color how the person operates in the world.

The next section describes the basic characteristics of each of the modalities. It's important to remember that people are more than their Sun signs and that most have all these modalities to a greater or lesser degree depending on the placement of all the planetary bodies.

Cardinal

The **cardinal modality** signs are Aries, Cancer, Libra, and Capricorn. These signs are initiating signs that love to take the lead and begin things and take action. They represent the project starter and are great at being the driver for new ideas but may lack follow-through to complete what they started. They will express themselves most through the element of their sign. For example, cardinal Aries is fire and is associated with being a very fast-moving self-starter.

The first day of each of the cardinal Sun signs coincides with the first day of each new season. The first day of Aries is the spring equinox (autumn in the southern hemisphere), Cancer is the summer solstice (winter in the southern hemisphere), Libra is the autumn equinox (spring in the southern

hemisphere), and Capricorn is the winter solstice (summer in the southern hemisphere).

Fixed

The **fixed modality** signs are Taurus, Leo, Scorpio, and Aquarius. These are the signs that fix ideas in place and do the work to manifest those ideas. The signs are hardworking and good at recognizing what needs to be done, coming up with a plan, and seeing it through to the end.

The fixed nature of these signs, however, can lead to rigidity and stubbornness—an unwillingness to be flexible—because they stay dedicated to the plan until completion.

The fixed signs fall in the middle of each season, a time when each season is at its peak and before beginning to shift to the next.

Mutable

Gemini, Virgo, Sagittarius, and Pisces are the **mutable modality** signs. Falling at the end of each season, they feel the pull to prepare for change. Mutable signs tie up loose ends, make adjustments, and prepare for the next change of season.

Flexibility and adaptability are the primary skills of mutable signs, and these are the signs that deal with unexpected shifts best. They are spontaneous and aim to find solutions to every twist in every plan. The downside of mutability is also their strength, as this much adaptability and willingness to change can lead to lack of commitment and flakiness.

THE FOUR ELEMENTS

The signs of the zodiac are further divided among the four elements—fire, air, earth, and water—and each element has three signs associated with it. Each of the elements is further associated with receptive or active energy, also often described as yin/yang, night/day, exhale/inhale, or feminine/masculine (though many astrologers are trying to move away from this language because of gender politics; planets, signs, and houses are ungendered).

Fire and air are active, yang, day, or inhale energy, and earth and water are receptive, yin, night, or exhale energy. As mentioned, three signs are associated with each element (also known as the **triplicities**). By combining the energy of the quadruplicities (or modalities) with the triplicities (or elements), you can begin to deepen your understanding of the complexity of your horoscope, and this will, thereby, deepen your tarot practice.

Fire

The three **fire signs** are Aries, Leo, and Sagittarius. The fire element is active, passionate, and both creative and destructive. Fire can burn everything to the ground but can also create heat and life force. This is the risk-taking element of the zodiac.

The fire element is enthusiastic and impatient, dynamic, temperamental, spontaneous, and pushy. Fire moves fast and burns out quickly, but it can also regenerate from the ashes, like the energy of the phoenix.

Earth

Taurus, Virgo, and Capricorn are the three earth signs. **Earth signs** are grounded, practical, solid, and dependable. This is the building energy of the zodiac—earth builds and makes things manifest, whether it's a physical building, a business, or worldly possessions. Earth energy can also be overly materialistic. Trees, plants, the ground we stand on are all of the earth element. Prudence and adversity to risk are also qualities of the earth signs.

Water

The three **water signs** are Cancer, Scorpio, and Pisces. This is the element associated with emotions, receptivity, fluidity, and creatively intuitive states. Water is flowing, sensitive, and compassionate, but can also be moody, self-indulgent, and prone to being out of touch with the real world. Conversely, the fantastical nature of water connects this element to music and art of all kinds, as a vivid imagination is associated with this element. Boundaries can also be problematic for water signs, as this element is associated with shape-shifting.

Air

Gemini, Libra, and Aquarius are the three **air signs**. Air is the element of the mind, communication, and ideas. Air signs love to analyze, think, speak, write, and synthesize information. Able to see other points of view, air signs make great mediators and collaborators, and they are more objective than signs corresponding with other elements.

Because of the ability to see all sides to any topic, air signs are more likely to blow hot and cold, and they are also likely to overthink, making them appear emotionally aloof at times. Air signs are, however, the most sociable signs of the zodiac.

THE PLANETS & LUMINARIES

Having covered the elements/triplicities and modalities/quadruplicities, we will move on to the individual planetary bodies in the cosmos. This section covers the **luminaries** (the Sun and the Moon) and the primary planets used in astrology, as well as those that have become associated with the Tarot.

Traditional astrologers tend to only study the planets up to and including Saturn (usually all called **personal planets** though Jupiter and Saturn are sometimes also called transpersonal planets) as they are the planets in our solar system that are visible to the naked eye. But most modern astrologers now include those beyond Saturn, or the **transpersonal planets** of Neptune, Uranus, and Pluto. Some astrologers also study asteroids and other newly discovered planetary bodies. Over time, you might want to expand your exploration of other planetary bodies and how to integrate them into your tarot practice. This isn't, however, necessary to gain a thoroughly robust and deep understanding of how to use astrology to enhance your tarot practice.

All the planets and both luminaries express themselves differently depending on the sign they are in at birth. The planetary bodies are the "what" (i.e., the Sun is the core, the Moon is the emotions, etc.), and the signs are the "how" (i.e., the ways in which they express themselves). For example, a Cancer Moon is very tender and protective, whereas a Moon in Aries is very emotionally direct and assertive.

The Sun

The Sun represents the core organizing principle of both our solar system and the self. It's our core or ego, our innate character. The Sun represents yang, day, and active energy.

The Sun is the ruler of the fire sign Leo and represents the heart, life, vitality, essence, and how you express your individuality. The Sun also represents creative potential. When it is well-expressed, it represents affection and joy. When it is less well-expressed, it can be overbearing and prideful. At the very core of being, the Sun is how we shine our light in the world—a pure and active outgoing expression of the self.

The Moon

Having no light of its own, the Moon is a receptive and reflective energy that responds and reacts. In our horoscope, the Moon represents the emotional body and moods, and rules the sign of Cancer.

The Moon represents inner and emotional security, with night or yin energy representing your relationship to family, home, nurturing, and the parent who "mothered" you.

The Moon rules the tides, our bodily cycles (including women's menstrual cycles), and our sleep cycles. Habits, memory, and our childhood conditioning are also realms of the Moon, as are our intuition and our subconscious feeling states or knowing.

Mercury

Mercury carries the shape-shifting energy of the deity who moved between the realm of the gods and humans. Mercury rules both night and day and the signs of Gemini and Virgo, air and earth signs, respectively.

Communication, detail, the mind, technical ability, perception, connection, and memory are all the realms of Mercury. As the closest planet to the Sun, the center of our solar system, Mercury is a messenger—the go-between for our core and the physical realm on Earth, making connections in reality and in the mind. As Mercury is a trickster/shape-shifter energy, it is very affected by the sign and house placement, but generally Mercury is curious and sociable and likes to have fun.

Venus

Venus is the planet of love, beauty, harmony, and manifestation. It rules both Libra, an air sign, and Taurus, an earth sign, and is therefore both day and night energy.

As the closest planet to Earth and the second from the Sun, Venus transmits our core values and our relationship energy through Mercury to our earthly selves. The Venus cycle aligns with the human gestation period, and the planet represents the Earth's (and humanity's) higher selves.

Expressed positively, Venus represents artistry, appreciation, aesthetics, money, banking, and our relationship to our senses—all that we can see, hear, smell, touch, and taste. At times, Venus can also be overly indulgent, greedy, vain, and lazy, but generally Venus seeks to express the higher vibrational qualities associated with love.

Mars

As the last of the planets known as the personal planets, Mars is the fourth "rock" from the Sun and stands guard as both protector and leader between the outer realms of the solar system and the other personal planets, and Earth. Unsurprisingly, as the outermost personal planet, Mars is representative of outer-world action and pioneering energy.

Life force, energy, passion, self-assertion, strength, anger, and animal instincts are the realm of Mars. As the ruler of Aries, Mars has very day, or yang, energy. However, Mars is also traditionally the ruler of Scorpio, and in that respect, also holds night energy and represents sexual passion, desire, willpower, willfulness, and survival instincts.

Jupiter

As we move away from the Sun, we move beyond the asteroid belt toward the social planets. The first of those is Jupiter, the planet of expansion and the urge to connect with the outer realms of the universe or something greater than ourselves.

Jupiter is ruler of the fire sign Sagittarius and holds day, or yang, energy. However, traditionally, Jupiter is also ruler of Pisces and therefore also has the dualistic quality of night, or yin, energy.

Jupiter represents fortune, expansion, belief, grace, seeking, joviality, aspirations, and abundance. Overextension, overconfidence, waste, and extremes are also the realm of Jupiter.

The guru, teacher, prophet, or hierophant are all represented by Jupiter, as are freedom, exploration of all kinds, and philosophy.

Saturn

The last of the planets visible to the naked eye is social Saturn. Traditionally thought to be the outer limit of our cosmos, Saturn represents limitations and restriction.

Saturn also has rulership of two signs, Capricorn (earth) and, traditionally, Aquarius (air) and has, therefore, qualities of both night/yin and day/yang energy.

Maturity, elderhood, healthy boundaries, prudence, patience, and mastery are represented by Saturn, as are fear, rigidity, and inhibition. Saturn rules the skeleton and bones, providing the framework of both the physical structures of the body and those we build. Achievement and effort provide the backbone to succeed and the resilience to climb whatever mountain sits before us.

Uranus

In 1781, the first of the transpersonal planets that are not visible to the naked eye was discovered and named after the sky god, Uranus. Uranus was given rulership to Aquarius (air) and, true to the boundary-shattering nature of its discovery, Uranus is the rule breaker, the rebel, and the revolutionary. It represents the urge for change, excitement, and liberation.

Breakdowns and breakthroughs are the domain of this day/yang energy. It also holds the energy of innovation, inspiration, and genius intelligence. This is the domain of eccentricity, individuality, and nonconformity. Science, inventions, and human connections in the wider sense are connected to Uranus. "Expect the unexpected" is a great expression for this restless, exciting, and unpredictable energy.

Neptune

In 1846, the second of the transpersonal planets—Neptune—was discovered by a mathematical prediction rather than empirical observation. This is reflective of the nebulous nature of the planet itself, which is named after the god of water and the sea, Neptune. We later discovered that Galileo observed Neptune in the 17th century, mistaking it for a star. Because confusion and elusiveness are associated with Neptune, the planet's very discovery reflects this.

Neptune rules oceanic Pisces (water) and represents the night/yin energy of oneness, mysticism, the muse, illusion and delusion, compassion, imagination, fantasy, and glamor. Transcendent states of oneness are also associated with Neptune, as are deception, unhealthy escapism, instability, loss of mental clarity, and addiction. Neptune is probably the most receptive and fluid of energies in the cosmos.

Pluto

Pluto is the last of the transpersonal planets used by most astrologers and associated with the Tarot. Pluto has been reclassified as a dwarf planet by astronomers following the discovery of a new class of dwarf planets. As more are discovered, their influence may be included in the evolving symbolism of the Tarot.

Pluto represents death, rebirth, and transformation; rules the sign of Scorpio; and therefore has a yin/night energy. Psychological depth and personal growth and soul evolution are the realms of Pluto, as are all realms that are hidden in the human psyche, especially around sexuality, desire, and intimacy. The shadow, repression, depression, and obsession are associated with Pluto, but so is the inner gold—the empowered part of the self that often remains hidden.

THE 12 HOUSES

Many elements make up the astrological chart. We've looked at the planets and the parts of the self, and now we'll look at the **12 houses**, which represent the areas of life experience, or where the planets operate strongly in the chart.

The 12 houses run counterclockwise around the chart and roughly follow a path of personal development from the first house (birth) to the twelfth house (metaphorical death and the time before birth). The first six houses are in the northern hemisphere of the chart, which is the bottom half from our perspective. They represent more personal, inner life experiences. Houses seven through twelve represent more interpersonal, public areas of life experience, making up the southern hemisphere of the chart.

By blending the planet and house meanings, we begin to get an understanding of the horoscope as a whole. After this section, we'll add in the signs, but please know that this is an overview meant to help you integrate this knowledge into your tarot practice.

The First House

Beginning at the ascendant or rising sign, which is the point on the eastern horizon at the moment of birth, the first house represents the persona or self.

How people see you initially, or what you project on first impression, such as your

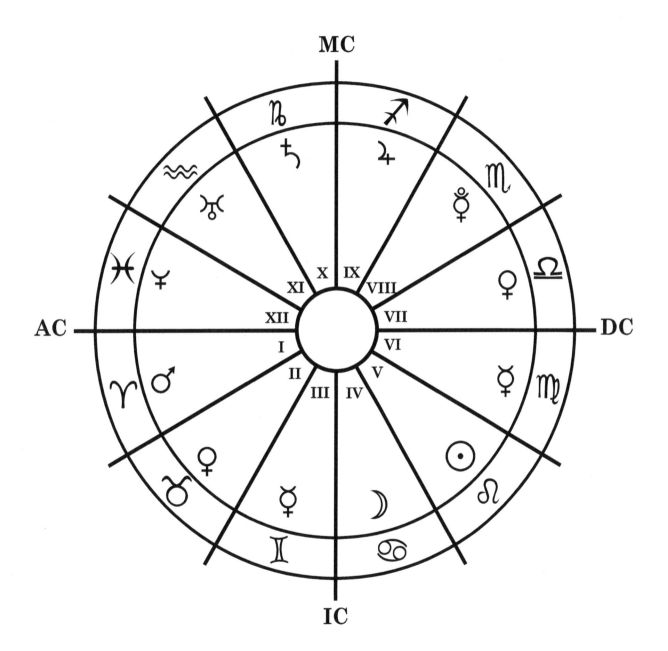

appearance, early abilities, birth experiences, and early childhood, are all represented by the first house. This is known as an **angular house**—the most powerful of houses—and is associated with Mars and Aries by most modern astrologers.

The Second House

The second house is the first of the **succedent** (middle in each quadrant of the horoscope and slightly less powerful than angular) houses. It represents personal resources of all kinds. This house is associated with Taurus and Venus.

Self-worth and self-esteem, personal possessions and what you value, your approach to earning and how you make your money, and your relationship to the body and the natural world are all associated with the second house.

The Third House

The first of the **cadent** (said to be least powerful) houses is the third house. It is ruled by Mercury and Gemini. This is the house of communication of all kinds.

This house represents communication and learning styles, perceptions, observation skills, and the gathering of information. Short journeys, siblings, local community, and neighbors are also represented here, as are gossip, emails, text messaging, and most social communication. Early education is also associated with this house.

The Fourth House

The fourth house is the house of the home and the second of the angular houses. This house represents not only our physical home, but also our home life, the type of home we prefer, and the most private parts of ourselves, the inner home.

Ruled by Cancer and the Moon, our emotional and material security is associated with this house. One of the parents is usually associated with it as well, alongside family of origin and ancestral traits and patterns. The fourth house represents self-care and how you fulfill your own emotional needs.

The Fifth House

Leo and the Sun rule the fifth house, a succedent house. This is the realm of self-expression and joy in life. All things fun are associated with the fifth house, including love affairs/romance, creativity, performing, sports, leisure, hobbies, play, and children.

This house represents any activity and form of expression that shines our light on the world, making it a sensitive house because others don't always show appreciation for the inner light of those around them.

The Sixth House

The sixth house is the realm of work/service and is a cadent house ruled by Mercury and Virgo. This is where we find meaning and the need to do activities that are useful in the world.

This house represents the nature of daily work and day-to-day routines. Health and pets are also grounded in the sixth house. As the last of the more personal houses before emerging into the interpersonal realms, this house is about wholeness. It's also about how you bring all of you together to be a contribution to the world and create balance—spiritually, mentally, and physically—to constantly refine and purify yourself.

The Seventh House

Venus and Libra rule the seventh house, an angular house. This house is about the outer world, or where we interact with others. Therefore, this house is about significant relationships, including the one with your partner.

The seventh house represents whom you attract and are attracted to, your patterns in significant relationships, and how you compromise yourself and your values for others—sometimes healthily, and sometimes not.

What Jung called "the disowned self" is also represented by the seventh house. This refers to the parts of the self that we don't like and that we see in others, triggering an emotional reaction of dislike.

The Eighth House

The eighth house is the house of intimacy and is a succedent house ruled by Pluto and Scorpio. This is the realm of true intimacy, deeply bonded relationships, and long-term partnerships that are connected sexually, psychologically, and emotionally. Merging of resources and life is also associated with the eighth house, which is why this is the house of shared finances and inheritances.

Magic and the occult, death (both physical and spiritual), sexual expression, and other topics that are often seen as taboo are all associated with the eighth house, as they are connected to deep intimacy with your soul.

The Ninth House

The higher self and all sources of expansion and inspiration are connected to the ninth house, which is a cadent house and is ruled by Jupiter and Sagittarius. Religion and personal experiences of the divine, all forms of higher study, whether formal or informal, and philosophy are all in the ninth house's realm.

Exploration of the world, other cultures, beliefs, knowledge, and the pursuit of truth, wisdom, and knowledge of natural law, along with freedom, are live in the ninth house. Travel, both physical and of the mind, also take residence here.

The Tenth House

The tenth house is last of the angular houses. It is found right at the top of the chart and represents the most public self. Saturn and Capricorn rule the tenth house.

This house is about how we are visible and vulnerable publicly because it represents how the world as a whole sees you and your reputation. This house also represents your mission and contribution to the world, which might just relate to your career. Because this house is your public status, there's a lot of energy around elder wisdom, integrity, responsibility, and duty.

As this is the polarity of the fourth house (the opposite house), one of the parents is also represented here—usually, the parent who represents the firm hand of authority and the one who is more out in the world.

The Eleventh House

The eleventh house is a succedent house and is ruled by Uranus and Aquarius. It represents community in a wider, more global sense than the local community of the third house. This is about large groups and organizations, often of intellectually like-minded people. It's also about the internet, communities, and associations/clubs.

Politics and social consciousness are the realm of the eleventh house, as are social and humanitarian causes. This is the house of hopes, wishes, and long-term goals for the future, of discoveries, and new ideas. It's also the house of the "big message" you have to share with the world.

The Twelfth House

The last cadent house is the twelfth house, which is ruled by Neptune and Pisces. This is the house of the unconscious—the realm of dreams, channeled creativity, psychism, and altered states.

The twelfth house is a place of mystery, magic, and mysticism, and also a place of fear of the nebulous. It was traditionally called the house of hidden enemies because we don't see people clearly in this house. Secluded places and seclusion are also associated with the twelfth house, including monasteries, retreat centers, prisons, and hospitals.

The amniotic fluid of the prenatal experience is associated with this watery realm, as is transpersonal knowledge.

THE 12 ZODIAC SIGNS

After discussing the planets, luminaries, and houses, we'll next look at the 12 signs. The signs in the horoscope are how each planet operates in the chart and the 30-degree divisions of the Sun's apparent annual path along the ecliptic. This is also known as the zodiac, or circle of animals, and is thought to date back to around 5000 BCE in ancient Babylon.

The zodiac signs are also known as Sun signs because they correspond to the Sun's apparent path. Each person has a Sun sign—the sign the Sun was in on the day of birth. However, the horoscope has all 12 zodiac signs, and each planetary body will be placed in a sign in the horoscope.

The Sun sign represents our core self or our intrinsic personality. In this section, we'll look at those traits, keywords, and ruling planets, but please remember that the key here is the blending of the planet, the "what," with the sign, or how that planet operates, and the house, or the area of life in which that planet operates. However, for the purposes of using astrology with the Tarot, an understanding of the energies of each sign is all that's required at first.

♈ Aries

The first sign of the zodiac, generally seen as the start of the astrological wheel and year, is Aries (approximately March 21 to April 20). Aries is a cardinal sign related to fire and day/yang energies. It is the pioneer of the zodiac. Symbolized by a ram, the Aries glyph represents the ram's horns. The sign is ruled by Mars.

This is "I am" energy—active, adventurous, assertive, and ardent. Aries energy is very direct and fast moving, and can be selfish, demanding, and aggressive at times. Aries is a sign of leadership and takes initiative, but it can also be highly competitive, as those born under this sign like to be first in all things.

♉ Taurus

The second sign of the zodiac is Taurus (approximately April 21 to May 20). It is a fixed sign with earth and night/yin energy. It is ruled by Venus. The symbol for Taurus is the bull, and the glyph represents the bull's head and horns. Taurus likes the physical world of the senses and likes to be surrounded by nice things, such as decadent food, a comfortable home, and a garden, as well as all the material possessions that appeal to them.

Taurus is steadfast, though sometimes stubborn, and can be possessive. Taurus represents embodiment and self-indulgence, and generally loves physical affection.

♊ Gemini

Gemini (approximately May 21 to June 20) is the third sign of the zodiac. It is a mutable sign associated with air and yang/day energies. It is ruled by shape-shifter Mercury. Gemini is the curious thinker of the zodiac, always taking in information, questioning, and talking about everything. Known as the sign of the twins, this imagery reflects the duality of this changeable sign, as those born under it can be duplicitous at times.

Gemini is sociable, chatty, cunning, mentally agile, and interested in anything and everything. This can mean they are the gossips of the zodiac. Gemini is very busy and adaptable, and often has a very nervous energy. Writing is associated with this sign.

♋ Cancer

The fourth sign of the zodiac is Cancer (approximately June 21 to July 20). It has a night/yin energy and is a cardinal, water sign ruled by the Moon. The symbol for Cancer is the crab, which feels safe and secure in its own shell. Cancer is all about feelings, family, and moods. Cancer is empathic, nurturing, and, at times, an emotionally needy sign.

People born under this sign are usually very protective of those they love, and that can be seen as smothering by less-needy signs. Home-loving Cancers like to cook—mostly comfort food—and feed others, as they are the caretakers of the zodiac. Cancers can also be moody, but they are also surprisingly tenacious, self-loving, and creative.

♌ Leo

Leo (approximately July 21 to August 20) is the fifth sign of the zodiac, and its symbol is the Lion. Leo is a fixed, fire, day/yang sign and loves to be in the spotlight and being showered with recognition. Leo rules the heart and is ruled by the Sun, and both these associations reflect the courageous, affectionate, and vital energy of Leo.

Because of Leo's love of adulation, they can be overbearing, lazy, and overly dramatic, especially if they aren't getting the attention they desire. A happy Leo is joyful, enthusiastic, playful, and very warm in nature.

♍ Virgo

The sixth sign of the zodiac is Virgo (approximately August 21 to September 20). It is a mutable earth sign with night/yin energy and is ruled by Mercury. Virgo is a service-oriented, analytical sign, and is symbolized by the maiden or virgin, which represents wholeness. It has a humble, reserved, and discriminating energy.

Virgo rules practicality, the crafts, hard work, organization, and efficiency. Virgo has a purity about it bordering on perfectionism and is very concerned with self-improvement. The analytical nature of those born under this sign can also lead to analysis paralysis and to being highly critical of themselves and others. Virgo's greatest desire is to be useful in the world.

♎ Libra

Air sign Libra (approximately September 21 to October 20) is the seventh sign of the zodiac. It is a cardinal sign with day/yang energy and is ruled by Venus. Libra is symbolized by the scales and represents balance and harmonization of opposites. Those born under the sign of Libra are the diplomats of the zodiac but can also be codependent, as they constantly attempt to achieve harmony.

Libra is charming, companionable, and idealistic—almost always pleasant to be around—but can also be self-absorbed and passive-aggressive, as they dislike conflict. This also means they can be fence sitters and find it difficult to make decisions. In general, Libras are peace-loving and creative, and love beauty and elegance.

♏ Scorpio

Scorpio (approximately October 21 to November 20) is the eighth sign of the zodiac. It has a night/yin energy, is a fixed water sign, and is ruled by Mars traditionally and Pluto in modern astrology. Scorpio is represented by the scorpion, the snake/serpent, and the eagle or phoenix, and these offer a great indicator about the depth of this sign.

Deep emotional transformation, passion, and desire are all associated with Scorpio. Scorpio is magnetic, brooding, compulsive, instinctual, and psychological. Scorpio can sting others with their intensity, as they are able to penetrate any artifice and uncover hidden motivations. Scorpios carry a secretive, unshakeable, and mysterious air. There's nothing light and fluffy about Scorpio energy.

♐ Sagittarius

The ninth sign of the zodiac is Sagittarius (approximately November 21 to December 20). It is a mutable fire sign with day/yang energy. It is ruled by Jupiter. Sagittarius is the wonderer and wanderer of the zodiac. Represented by the centaur archer, Sagittarius is constantly seeking—truth, new experiences, new knowledge, new cultures, new adventures, and new quests—and to integrate the human experience with higher spiritual ideals.

This is an aspirational sign that is, at times, reckless and careless in the rush to explore new horizons and freedom. Occasionally dogmatic and preachy, those born under this sign also usually do everything with good-natured humor. Sagittarius's blunt honesty isn't always welcome, as they can be tactless, but their optimism is infectious and inspirational.

♑ Capricorn

Capricorn (approximately December 21 to January 20) is the tenth sign of the zodiac. This achievement-oriented sign is a cardinal earth sign with night/yin energy. It is ruled by Saturn. Capricorn tends to be the late bloomer of the signs and can be very serious at a young age. Capricorn is reserved, conservative, hardworking, diligent, and very determined.

As an earth sign, however, Capricorn is also sensual and down to earth, and often has a very dry sense of humor that takes many by surprise, as the warm side of the Capricorn person is often hidden behind a serious demeanor. Capricorns generally become very wise elders and are good leaders. They are

often entrepreneurial in business as well as reliable, punctual, and efficient.

♒ Aquarius

Aquarius is the eleventh sign of the zodiac (approximately January 21 to February 20). It is a fixed air with day/yang energy. It is ruled by both Uranus and Saturn, traditionally. Aquarius is a mix of odd conservatism and ultra-modern. Aquarius is a paradox, inventive and intellectual and usually unusual. Aquarius has the ability to rise above and see the bigger picture, and the sign is associated with long-term future goals or hopes and wishes.

Aquarius is a revolutionary sign associated with altruism, social consciousness, and humanitarian causes. Emotionally distant, Aquarius often feels alienated from the world around them, and this, conversely, draws them to try to fit in. However, they are truly individuals who are best served by embracing their uniqueness.

♓ Pisces

Pisces (approximately February 21 to March 20) is the twelfth and final sign of the zodiac. A mutable water sign with a night/yin energy, it is ruled by Jupiter traditionally and Neptune in modern astrology. Pisces is an adaptable, dreamy, nebulous, and escapist sign that is all about faith and belief. Compassionate and empathic, this sign desires oneness and is highly sensitive to everything, so it is also associated with undefinable fears.

The malleable and impressionable energy of Pisces can make those born under this sign vacillating and vague at times, but overall, this is a kind, vulnerable, and idealistic sign that desires universality, love, and healing for the suffering in the world.

UNDERSTANDING ASTROLOGY WILL ADD A NEW LAYER OF INSIGHT TO THE CARDS

I invite you to read through the modalities, elements, planets, houses, and signs more than once, allowing yourself to gain a real feel for the different energies. The more you practice, the deeper your understanding will be. Perhaps even use a journal to note keywords that resonate for you, because writing often helps integrate learning more than by just reading.

Get to know the ruling planets of the signs and the connections between houses and signs. You will begin to see this imagery reflected in the Tarot, gaining deeper insight into the meaning of each card.

Both tarot and astrology can help you gain insight into yourself and your life. There's a lot to learn, but I want to emphasize that these insights will deepen over time as you intuitively tune in to the astrological imagery in the Tarot. The words contained in this book are a springboard to your understanding and not a definitive "how-to."

CONCLUSION

In this chapter, we looked at the basics of astrology. The aim of this book is to give you an understanding of the astrology within the imagery of the Tarot, not to teach you to read an astrology chart. If you would like to pursue astrology in greater depth, I suggest you explore my two previous books, *The Complete Guide to Astrology* and *Modern Astrology*.

Tarot is more of an intuitive divinatory tool than astrology, which is based on observance of the planetary movements and a long history of meaning, making it more accessible. Both work well together, however, in so many ways. Astrological symbolism and knowledge deepen tarot readings, and tarot can be used to add an extra layer of insight to astrological readings. You might just find that you pursue greater understanding of both over time. However, as you move on to the next chapter, you will explore the relationship between the Tarot and astrology.

3

ENHANCING YOUR TAROT PRACTICE WITH ASTROLOGY

In this chapter, you'll take a look at some of the influences in the Tarot, such as the Qabalah, before beginning to study the astrology within each card and then actually reading the cards through the lens of astrology. You'll expand on these areas throughout the book and will study the tarot cards in more depth as you go. I again invite patience and practice as you allow the knowledge and understanding to grow within you and your tarot reading.

TAROT & ASTROLOGY CAN WORK IN TANDEM TO DEEPEN YOUR PRACTICE

Although this book is about learning to integrate astrology into your tarot practice, the two can be used in tandem in so many ways. Tarot spreads for planetary cycles or the new or full moon, for example, are fairly common. Once you learn to integrate the two, you may find yourself creating your own tarot spreads and readings intuitively based on other cycles. Understanding the current planetary energies at a basic level also allows you to read the Tarot through that lens once you understand the astrological symbolism within the cards.

Similarly, the Tarot can be used to deepen astrological readings, such as by pulling a card for a powerful personal astrological aspect or transit. To provide astrological guidance using only the Tarot, simply pull a card for each sign on a new moon. The possibilities are endless. Follow what intuitively feels right for your tarot practice.

A Brief History of the Order of the Golden Dawn

Much of what we know of tarot today was developed through the Hermetic Order of the Golden Dawn. A. E. Waite, Aleister Crowley, and Pamela Colman Smith, the artist for the Rider-Waite Tarot, were all members.

The order was formed in 1888 by three Freemasons: William Robert Woodman, William Wynn Westcott, and Samuel Liddell "MacGregor" Mathers. Though only in existence until 1901, the Order of the Golden Dawn became one of the most influential hermetic (relating to an ancient occult tradition encompassing alchemy, astrology, and theosophy) societies in the 19th century, a time of increased interest in the exploration of the occult as an alternative to conventional religion.

The order studied symbolism derived from Jewish, Christian, and pagan mythology, combined with science, spiritualism, and magic derived from alchemical traditions, to create rituals designed to raise consciousness and help members attain a higher level of spiritual enlightenment through ritual and experiential initiation, not the worship of deities.

The Influences of Qabalah & the Tree of Life

The Qabalah is a Jewish mystical tradition that, like the Tarot, has a strong visual aspect, which is represented by the Tree of Life. The Tree of Life image contains 10 numbered circles (the same number as the cards in the

Minor Arcana of the Tarot) known as sephi-roth, meaning glowing sapphires. Each circle is said to represent an aspect of God.

The circles are connected by 22 numbered paths, and there are 22 letters in the Hebrew alphabet. Both are said to contain all of life within these paths and letters. The 22 paths have been assigned to the 22 tarot trump cards, or Major Arcana, by various authors. The Hebrew alphabet is displayed on the Major Arcana cards of the Thoth Deck.

Most consider the influence of the Qabalah and Tree of Life to be that of shared symbolism, although some practitioners believe there to be ancient origins to the relationship.

USING ASTROLOGY & TAROT TOGETHER WILL GIVE YOU MORE TOOLS FOR GROWTH

In this section, we'll take a look at how using tarot and astrology together will give you more tools for personal growth and development.

First, any study of the symbolism contained within the Tarot will strengthen your understanding, and studying the astrological elements and correspondences within the Tarot is such a major part of the symbolism that this alone will soon increase the depth of your practice. Just having a basic understanding of the elements, for example, will help you instantly see if a reading is more related to material (pentacles), emotional (cups), mental (swords), or transformative action (wands) matters. This will improve your reading of the cards beyond keywords and the imagery of the cards.

Understanding astrology will also boost your understanding of the archetypes contained within the Tarot. The symbolism of those archetypes will begin to speak to you at a higher level, and that will only add to the use of the Tarot for personal growth. The astrology will also provide additional guidance beyond the imagery of the cards alone, and that will further provide guidance for life choices and help you navigate wins and losses.

As you study the cards alongside this book, you will, over time, seamlessly read the cards through the rich lens of astrology, and because astrology is one of the most powerful tools for personal growth there is, this can only make your tarot practice more powerful.

TAROT & YOUR NATAL CHART

Can I use a tarot reading to gain insights into my natal chart? How do I do that?

Yes! There are many ways you can use tarot to gain insight into your natal chart. You could create a spread that asks for guidance for each planetary placement, such as the Sun in Leo, the Moon in Gemini, Mercury in Cancer, and so on. Additionally, you could add in the house placements and angles, your ascendant, midheaven, descendant, and Imum Coeli (where the ecliptic in space crosses the meridian toward the north in the skies), perhaps by laying the cards out around a printout of your natal chart. You could also do house placements only or a spread based on the signs on the house aspects.

LET'S EXPLORE THE TAROT USING ASTROLOGY

Now that you have gained a basic understanding of the signs, planets, and houses, it's time for an overview of the Major Arcana, the suits, and the trumps, plus a quick look at the numbers. The second part of this book will include even more details, but let's start here.

THE MAJOR ARCANA

The 22 cards of the Major Arcana (mysteries) in the Tarot are the trump cards and are the most impactful of the cards as, even though archetypes are contained in all cards, these are archetypal images that follow the soul journey through life and personal growth. This is known as the Fool's journey. Spend a good deal of time getting to know the Major Arcana and the astrological symbolism contained in these cards.

Each card of the Major Arcana is associated with a planet or sign. In some decks, the astrological glyphs are on the cards; the Thoth Deck, for example, has them on most cards. However, the symbols do not appear on all decks, so it's helpful to understand the symbolism yourself rather than rely on the glyphs. It's also helpful to have only the Major Arcana cards in front of you while you study so you can see how one card leads to another in the spiritual journey of personal growth.

The Fool/Uranus

The Fool is card zero, the infinite potential at the start of the soul's journey. This card is associated with the planet Uranus, who in the pantheon of the gods was Father Sky and creator of all life with Gaia, the Earth. The appearance of the Fool card is a call to be open to anything in the path of life. Uranus, the bringer of awakening, surprise possibilities, and lightning bolts reflects the unconstrained potential contained in the Fool. Like Uranus, the Fool asks for spontaneity, a free spirit, and expecting the unexpected. Both the Fool and Uranus are exciting energies, full of untapped potential on life's journey, and all the elements are contained in the whole of this card.

The Magician/Mercury

Major Arcana card one, the number of beginnings, is associated with the messenger of the gods, Mercury, bringing information from the heavens to Earth and vice versa. Both Mercury and the Magician are jugglers, connecting different elements to create magic. All the elements are reflected in the Magician card, and this card represents the intention or ability to actually create magic using the tools, skills, and resources available to you—in other words, to make your ideas manifest into reality. Mercury moved between the gods and humans, and this represents the Magician's intention to connect the spirit and physical realms to create magic.

The High Priestess/Moon

The High Priestess is the card numbered two—the number of relationships and diplomacy—in the Major Arcana and is associated with the Moon. Both the Moon and this card are connected to our intuitive and emotional connection to spirit and each other, and to our inner wisdom. This card is also primarily associated with the element of water. Both the Moon and the High Priestess are powerful energies of creation, sometimes referred to as the divine feminine, which exists within us all. When this card appears, we are being asked to trust our inner wisdom and to pay attention to our feelings, dreams, and meditative messages.

The Empress/Venus

The Empress is the card numbered three, the number of creative self-expression and natural rhythm, in the Major Arcana. It is associated with Venus in her earthly, Taurean energy of sensuality, core values, and the higher self. When this card appears, it's a call to connect with earthly energy, get grounded, and tap into motherly, compassionate love, showing that love to yourself and the world around you. It may also represent a motherly figure in your life whose support you need.

The Emperor/Aries

The Emperor is card number four in the Major Arcana, the number of conscientious responsibility. It is associated with Aries, the leader of the zodiac and a passionate fire sign. Embodiment of a more dominant, powerful energy is called for when this card appears. This can represent either seeking out the support of a strong, powerful person or finding that energy within yourself. This card calls for structure, control, and stability, and could be seen as a father figure or type of person with great inner strength.

The Hierophant/Taurus

In ancient times, a hierophant was the interpreter, or revealer, of sacred mysteries and esoteric principles. The Hierophant card is numbered five in the deck. This is the number of change, divine grace, and the mind. This card is associated with Taurus, a receptive, stable, and self-indulgent earth sign, which suggests that this card is about receiving and interpreting divine grace so that we understand how to live as humans in the material world. It's about understanding and living within well-established principles and values, as reflected by the fixed and steadfast quality of Taurus. In a reading, the card can also suggest a spiritual counselor type of figure who can help the querent understand and make sense of their lives.

The Lovers/Gemini

Card number six, the number of harmony and idealism, is the Lovers card and is associated with the sign of Gemini. Both the Lovers card and Gemini represent the twins, the union of opposites, relationships, and choices. Gemini and this card are both about the union of opposites within the mind and the choices to be made to achieve harmonious connections in all relationships, whether with others or with your earthly and spiritual desires. This card appears when there are decisions or compromises to be made.

The Chariot/Cancer

The Chariot is numbered seven, the number of introspection and reclusiveness, in the Major Arcana. It is connected to the sign of Cancer. Like the sign of Cancer, this card is all about gathering your willpower and strength to overcome challenges and take control. The Chariot card draws upon the tenacity of the sign of Cancer, inviting you to overcome distractions to focus and move forward with determination and self-discipline.

Strength/Leo

Number eight, the number of perfect balance, goes to the Strength card. It is associated with Leo, the sign ruled by the Sun, our core. Leo rules the heart and courage ("heart" is *cœur* in French), and as this suggests, this card represents acting with heart, from a place of core strength. In the Thoth Deck, this is the Lust card, in reference to having a lust for life, reflecting the energy of Leo. When this card appears, you are being asked to operate from your heart and with confidence and true inner power. Passion, desire, and creative self-expression are all indicated by this card.

The Hermit/Virgo

In the Major Arcana, the card numbered nine, the number of wisdom and responsibility, is the Hermit. It is associated with the humblest of signs, Virgo. As discussed in the previous chapter, Virgo is a sign of wholeness, of being reserved and discriminating, and acting in service to others. Like the sign of Virgo, the Hermit is about shining a light inward. Virgo's planet is Mercury, the planet of the mind. It is about learning about the self and self-improvement, so the Hermit card invites you to spend time on inner contemplation.

The Wheel of Fortune/Jupiter

Jupiter, the planet of fortune, expansion, and growth, is associated with the number 10, the number of fortunate new beginnings, in the Major Arcana. This card is the Wheel of Fortune. Jupiter cycles are 12 years long, and when Jupiter returns to the point it was when a person was born, called the Jupiter return, people can expect a period of change and personal growth, which is reflected in the Wheel of Fortune card. Around the age of 12, for example, we move into the teen years of learning to become adults, and around age 24, many of us leave college and enter the world of work. Both Jupiter and the Wheel of

Fortune represent new beginnings, change, life cycles, luck, and fortune.

Justice/Libra

The Justice card is numbered 11 in the Major Arcana, the karmic master teacher number. It is associated with Libra, the sign of balance, justice, and harmony. Libra is an air sign, and therefore, this card is also associated with mediation and diplomacy, both skills that are connected to justice. Accountability and consequences are reflected in the Justice card and the sign of Libra. Both are connected to the scales symbol and bringing balance after the period of growth reflected by the Wheel of Fortune card.

The Hanged Man/Neptune

Neptune is an energy of dissolution, of letting go and letting God, and is associated with number 12, the number of completions of a cycle of life experience. It is also the Hanged Man in the Major Arcana. The Hanged Man represents trust and surrender, along with connection to source energy and not holding on too tightly to the material realm. The energy of both Neptune and the Hanged Man reflects uncertainty, indecision, and nebulousness, and calls for patience rather than forcing decisions.

Death/Scorpio

Number 13, the most feared number and the number of upheaval and the goddess, is the most feared card in the Major Arcana. It is known as the Death card and is connected to the deepest of signs, Scorpio. Both Scorpio and this card represent death, rebirth, and transformation. In truth, though, it refers to a psychological or spiritual death and rebirth resulting from profound changes. Because change of this proportion is usually uncomfortable, yet part of the Fool's journey through life, there is often fear around this card.

Temperance/Sagittarius

The Temperance card is numbered 14, the number of unity and prudence, in the Major Arcana. It is connected to the sign of Sagittarius. The symbol for Sagittarius is a centaur/archer, and this reflects the call in the Temperance card to balance the subconscious with the material world and to integrate all dualities in our nature. Sagittarius is the seeker of truth and desires to integrate the human experience with higher spiritual ideals in a balanced union.

The Devil/Capricorn

In the Major Arcana, the Devil or Capricorn card is numbered 15, the number of spirited guts and passion with a tough outer shell. Both Capricorn and the Devil have complex symbology. The secret to understanding this is knowing that Capricorn is, at heart, a sensual Earth sign that has a devilish side hidden behind a serious exterior. This is reflected in the sea goat symbol for Capricorn—the body of a goat and tail of a fish—suggesting that hiding behind a fearful, determined, and ambitious exterior is a different person. Understanding this enables us to see the Devil card as representing our own limiting beliefs, fears, and blocks around our own deeper, earthy instincts.

The Tower/Mars

The card numbered 16, the number of strength of will, is the Tower in the Major Arcana. Mars's relationship to the card is that of cutting out the old (Mars rules knives and sharp objects) and starting the new. That could include new projects, new relationships, and new cycles. Mars also represents action, and when change calls, action is needed, as are willpower, assertion, and strength to release that which needs to be left behind as you make a fresh start.

The Star/Aquarius

The Star card is number 17, a highly spiritual number. In the Major Arcana, it is associated with Aquarius, the sign of future goals, hopes, and wishes. The sign of Aquarius connects the dots of the bigger message of the universe and the planets, bringing innovative and sometimes revolutionary ideas to Earth in a practical way, as reflected by the energies of Aquarius's corulers, Uranus (innovation) and Saturn (practical), and the symbolism of the card itself, which shows the connectedness of bringing spirit and ideas to Earth.

The Moon/Pisces

Card number 18, the number of inner emotional strength, is the Moon card. It is associated with the compassionate and empathic sign Pisces. Pisces is a sign of duality—of fear and longing, and of faith and lack of faith. As a nebulous, unclear energy, it points to uncertainty about the path ahead, which is reflected in the Moon card. Illusion, uncertainty, and subconscious fears are associated with the card. Understanding the indecisive, adaptable, escapist energy of Pisces can help you understand its meaning.

The Sun/Sun

The Sun, card number 19, represents the alpha and omega number of the circle of life. It is tied to the astrological Sun, our core, life force, and the central organizing principle of the solar system and living things. As the Sun invites us to shine our light, the card represents optimism, vitality, joy, confidence, and happiness radiating outward.

Judgment/Pluto

Card number 20, the number of understanding of good and evil, is the Judgment card. It is associated with Pluto, the planet of transformation, death and rebirth, and transition. The Judgment card reflects the end or completion of a cycle or phase of life before a new beginning. As each stage of life or cycle comes to an end, there's a review of what's working and that which needs to be cleared away, and this is Pluto's role. Pluto excavates what isn't working and, as such, is associated with elimination and judging what is and isn't needed moving forward.

The World/Saturn

The final card in the Major Arcana is number 21, the number of growth, and is associated with Saturn, the planet of mastery, maturity, and achievement. Saturn's cycle of 29 years is connected with the graduation from one life cycle to another, from youth to maturity to elderhood. The World card reflects this Saturnian theme. When this card appears, it suggests a cycle has been completed, that congratulations are in order, and that your fear of not being enough were unfounded. It's time for a pat on the back.

THE MINOR ARCANA

There are 56 Minor Arcana (mysteries) cards in tarot decks, and they are divided into four suits: cups, pentacles, wands, and swords. Each of the four suits contains 10 numbered cards and four court cards: the Page, Knight, Queen, and King.

Minor Arcana cards generally represent a temporary influence that is moving through life at the time of the reading, whereas the Major Arcana represents bigger archetypal themes influencing life's journey. This does not mean that the Minor Arcana is lesser in influence; they just operate in different ways.

Because the Minor Arcana cards represent a more temporary influence, they offer insight into how current situations are impacting a person and guidance around how to work with the influence and the situation. The Minor Arcana, in essence, deals with the practicalities of daily life, whereas the Major Arcana represents bigger archetypal themes.

Each of the Four Suits Corresponds to an Element

As discussed in the previous chapter, the zodiac signs are all connected to the four elements: water, earth, fire, and air. This is the same for the Minor Arcana cards of the Tarot, with each suit associated with one of the four elements. By really starting to understand the astrological and energetic meaning of the different elements, your understanding of the tarot will deepen over time and you will, at a glance, understand whether a spread is most concerned with, for example, relationships or career and money.

CUPS (WATER/WATER SIGNS)
The cups suit is represented by the element of water and the astrological signs Cancer, Scorpio, and Pisces. It is therefore associated with emotional and creative matters. This could be about your emotional life and/or your emotional connection and response in relationships.

PENTACLES (EARTH/EARTH SIGNS)
The earth element and the astrological signs Taurus, Virgo, and Capricorn represent the suit of pentacles. All earthly and more mundane matters, such as finances, possessions, careers, nature, and the body, are associated with these cards.

SWORDS (AIR/AIR SIGNS)
The suit of swords is represented by the element of air and the astrological signs Gemini, Libra, and Aquarius. Swords represent ideas, thoughts, words, and actions. This can mean anything from communicating your ideas to facing decisions and speaking your truth.

WANDS (FIRE/FIRE SIGNS)
The fire element and the astrological signs Aries, Leo, and Sagittarius represent the wands suit. Like the fire signs, this suit is associated with action, passions, and motivation. Inspiration, creative self-expression, and spirituality are also connected to this suit.

The Court Cards Also Correspond to the Elements

Like the suits, the court or trump cards also correspond to the elements. Because tarot reading, like astrology, means combining different layers of meaning and symbolism to create a coherent story, you may, for example, have a court card that is a double Earth—both from an Earth suit and an Earth court card, or a court card that is a combination of elements.

When a card is a combination of elements, think about how the two elements work together in our environment. Wind fans the flames of fire, whereas water and earth create mud. Fire and water do not complement each other, and neither do earth and air, so there is more tension. Whereas fire and earth complement each other in a more balanced way, as do air and water. This is like combining the modalities and elements in astrology to build layers of understanding.

PAGES (EARTH)

The Pages court cards, known as the Princess cards in some decks, correspond to the element of earth. As earth is a very tangible element, this can represent a part of the self or another person that is creating something stable and "real," the beginning of something new.

KNIGHTS (AIR)

Traditionally the Knights court cards correspond to the element of air. However, some associate Knights with fire, so I invite you to come to your own correspondence after working with the cards. Air is a very fresh element that corresponds to forward thinking and movement and that applies to the Knight cards.

QUEENS (WATER)

Water is the element corresponding to the Queens court cards. Water is a nurturing, feeling element that is connected to sustainability and sustenance. This is the court card of emotional intelligence, which also corresponds to the water element.

KINGS (FIRE)

Some practitioners see the Kings cards as corresponding to air, but traditionally, fire is associated with the Kings cards. I again invite you to explore both possibilities for yourself. The fire element and astrological signs are often associated with leadership, success, and action, as well as with making an impact on the world.

The Numbered Cards Have Their Own Associations

We've looked at elements in the Minor Arcana, but the card numbers also have their own associations, which can add another layer of interpretation to your readings when paired with the element of the suit. The numbers carry a common meaning across the suits and are as follows:

1/ACE	New Beginnings
2	Balance
3	Creation
4	Foundation
5	Change
6	Harmony
7	Reflection
8	Mastery
9	Accomplishment
10	Completion

The Role of Decans

Each astrological sign equals 30 degrees, and each sign can be further divided into 10-degree portions called **decans**. Each decan of the zodiac has a tarot card correspondence, beginning at the Aries/Mars decan (the first decan) and the two of wands, a cardinal fire sign and card. All cardinal sign decans begin at two of the corresponding suit and element. Fixed signs correspond to the middle three numbers, and mutable signs to the last three numbers.

THE MINOR ARCANA CARDS EACH CORRESPOND TO A HOUSE & SIGN

Like the decans, each Minor Arcana card corresponds to an astrological house and sign. You can find these correspondences by combining elements and qualities. The aces do not have a corresponding house and sign, however, as they are said to represent the entire element and, therefore, all three signs and houses associated with each element.

Cardinal signs—Aries, Cancer, Libra, and Capricorn—all correspond to cards numbered two, three, and four, as they are the initiating, or first, numbers. These cards also correspond to the angular houses, the first in each quadrant.

Cards five, six, and seven correspond to the fixed signs—Taurus, Leo, Scorpio, and Aquarius—and the succedent houses, two, five, eight and eleven.

Cadent houses, three, six, nine, and twelve, at the end of each quadrant, correspond to the mutable signs—Gemini, Virgo, Sagittarius, and Pisces—and the last three numbered cards of each suit.

THERE'S A LOT TO DISCOVER

You have probably realized by now that there's a lot to discover when applying astrology to your tarot practice. And yet, this is only the beginning. Don't get overwhelmed! Your depth of understanding will continue to grow, and each time you return to a section of this book, you may discover something new.

Take it slowly, learn with your tarot deck in hand, and let the understanding build. Try separating out each Arcana and suit, then the numbered cards together, and just study the cards alongside this book. Some people find journaling about each card to be helpful. Journal about the element, the decan, the sign, the house, the archetypes, and the meaning as related to specific cards. Choose your own language to describe the energy of the cards. Most important, trust your intuition to sense the meaning of each card and the astrological symbolism contained within it.

YOU WILL LEARN WITH PRACTICE

The more you learn and use the Tarot, the more you will understand. There is no finish line with either tarot or astrology, and the same applies to using both together. I learn something new every day in both arts, and the best way to integrate all that you are learning is to keep practicing.

Read for yourself daily, and practice on others. Remain open to new insights and changing perspectives. Not all tarot practitioners or astrologers agree on every detail, so know what your intuition ascertains is perfect for you.

CONCLUSION

We have now explored the basic history and meaning of astrology and tarot and begun to explore how the elements, modalities, planets, luminaries, houses, decans, and astrological symbolism and archetypes are reflected within the Tarot. The next chapter invites you to start reading the Tarot using the knowledge you have gained so far. You'll learn how to set up your environment, how to connect to the cards, how to prepare the deck, and, most important, how to read the cards using astrology.

4

READING YOUR CARDS THROUGH THE LENS OF ASTROLOGY

Now that you're gaining an understanding of the basics of both tarot and astrology, it's time to really begin to dive deep into how to read the cards through the lens of astrology. Remember, your understanding of the foundations of the cards, modalities, planets, luminaries, houses, and signs will grow over time. Have patience with yourself and allow yourself to tune in to the magic of the symbolism of the Tarot at an intuitive level. The descriptions and meanings covered so far are meant as a springboard for your own development, not as rigid rules. Also, remember that this book is not trying to teach you to be a professional astrologer, so avoid feeling overwhelmed by the depth of astrology.

APPLYING ASTROLOGY TO THE CARDS WILL OPEN UP A WHOLE NEW WORLD

Tarot decks usually come with a little book explaining what the cards mean. Although they can be useful, they rarely discuss the astrological and other symbolism of the cards. I invite you to move beyond rote learning. Get to know the elements, modalities, planets, signs, and houses. Play with the deck by laying out the different elements or other symbols. I have suggested keeping a journal, but that's not the only way to tune in. You can meditate on each card after reading the initial chapters of this book. The more you work with the cards, the more you will see in them. Don't worry about getting things "right," because tarot cards represent so much and speak to different things depending on the querent and their place in a spread. Allow yourself to build up the trust in your knowing after studying the basics.

PUT YOUR NEW KNOWLEDGE TO WORK

In the next sections, you'll learn about setting up your environment, connecting to the cards, and preparing your deck. You'll also learn about how to choose the right deck for you, the differences in reading for yourself and others, how to open and close a reading, and how to read the cards using what you have learned about astrology. A sample reading will help you see what you've learned in practice.

If you have cards you like at this point, great. Perhaps you can keep that deck on hand as you move through this chapter. If not, choose your deck using the tips in this chapter and gather the other resources you will need.

SET UP YOUR ENVIRONMENT

The environment in which you conduct tarot readings is a sacred space physically, mentally, emotionally, and spiritually, so create a space that works for you. A space that is noisy, distracting, and full of interruptions will not be conducive to tuning in to your intuition, which is what you are doing when you read the Tarot.

A physical space where you have privacy and no interruptions is ideal, whether you are reading for yourself or others. Even if you are reading in public spaces, try to create a feeling of privacy. A short breathing exercise or meditation is a good practice to prepare yourself mentally and emotionally, grounding you in the space of the Tarot. You might want a special reading cloth for your cards, as well as a few objects that have spiritual meaning for you, such as a crystal or two, incense, candles, pictures, and soothing music.

As always, your own intuition should guide you in creating the space, but aim for a calm, soothing, and centered feel.

CONNECT TO YOUR CARDS & PREPARE YOUR DECK

There is no "right" way to prepare your deck and to connect with your cards, so everything mentioned in this section is suggestion only. The important thing is that you do actually prepare in some way.

When you first open your deck, do so with reverence, feeling the cards in your hand, looking through them one by one, and connecting energetically. Choose a quiet place and moment, and approach your deck as you might approach a person, because you are going to develop a deep relationship with your cards. If, over time, you grow your tarot deck collection, you will notice that you have a different relationship to each deck.

Some people love to cleanse their deck by smudging with smoke incense or crystals, or by lighting a candle nearby and letting the candle burn off any unwelcome energies. Charging a deck, usually by placing it under the rays of a full moon, is another common practice. Some readers cleanse and charge every full moon. You may also choose to wrap your deck in a special cloth or keep it in a special bag. This is all personal preference.

OPEN YOUR MIND TO WHAT THE CARDS CAN TEACH YOU

This book will teach you the astrological connections and symbology of the cards, but this is only the beginning. What's most important when working with the Tarot is keeping an open mind regarding what the cards can teach you.

Think of your relationship with the cards as an interpersonal relationship. The cards speak to you as a person would, so learn to listen to them. Feel them, touch them, shuffle them, look at them, and get to know them intimately. The more you do this, the more

HOW TO CHOOSE THE RIGHT DECK FOR YOU

One of the biggest tarot fallacies, in my opinion, is that a deck should be gifted to you and not bought. I disagree with that and would only have one deck if that were the case. Many people would never get started with a tarot practice if they waited to be gifted a deck.

Choosing the right deck or decks is, again, highly personal. Look at the imagery; feel the weight of the cards and their quality. Do you prefer larger cards or not? Most important, the deck should speak to you. If buying online, perhaps search for images of all the cards to be sure that the whole deck speaks to you.

Be aware that there are also Oracle decks and other kinds of divination decks. If you are choosing to be a tarot reader, however, make sure to get a tarot deck with 78 cards. You might choose to use both in time, but this book is teaching you how to specifically read tarot through the lens of astrology.

Your first deck may not be your only deck. You may have several decks that each speak to you differently as you grow and develop your practice.

the cards will speak to you until you no longer need reference books or websites. The colors, shapes, numbers, and symbols will all begin to speak to you once you begin to integrate their basic meanings and astrological correspondences. The cards will become an extension of your inner knowing.

This is where the real magic lies, so have patience, practice, and know there is no final destination. Even the most experienced tarot practitioners learn or intuit new things all the time. This is a journey that deepens over time.

READING FOR YOURSELF VS. READING FOR OTHERS

You can read the Tarot for yourself as well as for others. However, it's important to be aware of the lack of objectivity when reading for yourself; there may be a temptation to shape the reading for the desired answer.

If you are reading for yourself, be very clear about your question and trust the cards that come up. Avoid second-guessing and searching for a different answer than the initial one, as the one you receive intuitively is always the one meant for you. Also, avoid using the cards as a crutch during times of anxiety or heightened emotions. That's the best time to get a reading from someone else.

When reading for others, take time to tune in to the cards' energy and to ask what guidance is sought. I find the best time to do that is when shuffling the cards.

OPENING A READING

As with any divinatory art, there is a lot of differing advice, from specific ways to shuffle the deck to tapping on the cards to clear the energy before shuffling. There is no right way. The following are only suggestions, so adapt them as feels right for you.

Prepare your space with music, incense, crystals, a candle, or other soothing, meditative objects.

Quiet your inner voice by closing your eyes, meditating, and saying a prayer or affirmation. This might include asking for permission to read for a client and for protection and guidance through the process.

Connect your energy field to the cards and shuffle, always treating your cards respectfully. Use any shuffle technique that works for you. If you are working with a client, visualize their energy also connecting with you and the cards. Perhaps ask their questions as you shuffle.

HOW TO READ THE CARDS WITH ASTROLOGY

Once you have opened the reading and pulled the cards, placing the chosen spread in front of you (we'll look at spreads in upcoming chapters), it's time to begin reading the cards using astrology.

The most important thing to consider first is the elements. Which element is prominent in the cards pulled? A lot of cups cards mean that the element of water is prominent and that matters of emotion and the heart are involved. A dominance of wands represents fire, inspiration, and transformation. Material matters would be primarily represented by pentacles, and if there are mainly swords, mental matters and decisions are likely prominent.

Next, look at the planets, signs, and houses associated with the cards and integrate the meanings into the insights gained from the cards' symbolism.

Over time, you might choose to develop your readings in association with the querents' astrological horoscope or chart, or the current planetary cycles and transits. For example, if you can see that a client is experiencing their first Saturn return around age of 29, you can ask the cards for guidance around that. The possibilities are endless.

CLOSING A READING

When a reading is complete, you may find that certain energies have accumulated around you. You may have also entered an altered state or very different state of mind. Closing a reading helps to bring you back to the present. Thank the cards and the universe/energies that have guided you in the reading with a short prayer or a few words. Then release these energies so they don't stay with you.

Finally, spend a few moments grounding your own energy by doing a short meditation or merely reconnecting with your physical self. You may also visualize a bubble or light of protection around you so that you don't carry any of the energies you picked up during the reading with you.

A SAMPLE READING

Now we move onto the exciting part, and what this book is all about, with a first sample reading. We're going to begin with a simple, one-card pull, highlighting the astrological elements in the card.

For this reading, I pulled the ace of wands. The suit of wands is the fire element, representing passion, inspiration, action, and spiritual transformation. Combine that with the number of the card and know that this is potential for new inspiration and spiritual growth. Perhaps consider that the number one represents the first sign, Aries, and first house, the beginning of the wheel of life.

This brings in the cardinal modality and an angular house, both representing the energy of new beginnings. A fiery new start of a project with Mars ruling Aries, this card suggests a real desire to take action.

Look closer at the elemental imagery in the card, however, and we see that the wand is held by a hand that looks like a cloud, and there are water, mountains, and a castle in the background. These bring in the elements of air, water, and earth, suggesting that the card requires bringing mind, body, and spirit into the creative potential.

BUILD A RELATIONSHIP WITH YOUR CARDS

At this point, consider pulling a daily card and making notes about what you see in the card. Refer to the chapters so far and look for the elements, numbers, planets, signs, and houses. This is all about building a relationship with your cards. Spend time with the cards, ask questions, listen with an open mind, and add to a tarot journal daily.

Repetition and practice really help to grow your relationship with the cards, and like any healthy long-term relationship, the more time spent connecting, listening, and conversing, the more the relationship grows and strengthens.

YOUR INSIGHTS WILL GROW WITH TIME

Time is your friend when it comes to tarot. That doesn't mean that your early readings and insights are not valuable. You may find yourself referring back to this book and your journal a lot early in your relationship with the cards. That's perfectly normal.

Over time, your insights will grow and become *your* insights, informed by the knowledge you have gained in this book. You will get to the point of trusting what the cards tell you by their placement in a spread, the questions asked, and the energies connecting you to the cards and the querent.

CONCLUSION

In this chapter, we have begun the process of learning to read the Tarot through the lens of astrology, building on the basics contained in earlier chapters. We've also looked at connecting to your cards, your environment, and opening and closing readings. It might be helpful to pause at this point and go over these early chapters with a journal to get to know each suit and card. Or you might prefer to move on and use the early chapters as a reference. Neither is the right way; do what works for you.

In the next chapter, you'll look at some sample readings. You'll look at the benefits of multi-card spreads, how to set up and interpret a spread through the astrological lens, view some sample spreads, and look at when and how you might go about creating your own spreads.

5

SAMPLE SPREADS & READINGS

In this chapter, you'll look at some sample spreads with step-by-step suggestions for how to read the spreads using the lens of astrology. You'll also learn about the benefits of a multi-card spread, how to set up and interpret spreads, and how to create your own spreads using the lens of the planets, luminaries, elements, signs, and houses. Take your time with each section, bring your cards to the table, and do your own practice spread alongside the sample spread. Make notes. You will soon start to see the astrological symbolism in the cards, the patterns, and how one card moves to the next. You will learn how to see the bigger picture before focusing on each individual card, and most important, you will build a relationship to the cards at every step.

TAROT & ASTROLOGY CAN OPEN YOUR MIND TO NEW POSSIBILITIES

Move beyond the information in books and learn to see the possibilities of your personal practice. I remember the moments in my own practice where astrology and the Tarot started to speak to me, and I no longer needed to look up what others had written. That doesn't mean you won't continue to learn from others—just that you will learn to trust what your intuition tells you.

You will eventually reach a point where the symbolism seems to leap out at you and you can see the patterns, colors, shapes and other symbolism. What you have learned will be so ingrained in your mind, body, and spirit that you may eventually feel as if the cards are an extension of your mind, body, and spirit and you will "receive" messages in a reading that seem to come from nowhere. You might see that as spirit messages or your inner knowing; it doesn't really matter where the messages come from.

Try to let go of thinking there is a right or wrong way to read the cards through the lens of astrology; the possibilities are endless.

A ONE-CARD PULL IS GREAT, BUT A SPREAD IS EVEN BETTER

In the previous chapter, you looked at a sample one-card spread. This is useful for yes-or-no type question or simple guidance for the day. I pull a card most days just for focus on the day's energies, where to apply myself, where I need to adjust, and what to be cautious of. One-card pulls are also wonderful for getting to know your cards. They can be used as a meditation tool and as a writing or journaling prompt. One-card pulls are focused, and you must look deeply at the symbolism in the pulled card without any supporting clarification.

A spread goes deeper and is different, though not necessarily better, despite the words I use in the section title. A spread offers detailed guidance. Each card in a spread builds on the other. The overarching elements contained in a spread can indicate where the querent needs guidance. The court cards can indicate supportive, or otherwise-influential, people who may not be supportive necessarily. And the Major Arcana can represent actual astrological transits the querent is experiencing. A spread can provide profound insights about the past, present, and future to guide the querent, just as an astrological reading alone can.

THE BENEFITS OF A MULTI-CARD SPREAD

Whereas a one-card pull is fabulous for a yes-or-no question or simple guidance around focus, a multi-card spread has many benefits that a one-card pull can't offer.

Most of us fear change. If you are going through a period of transition in your life, a multi-card spread can help to identify any blocks or unfinished business you may be encountering and can help you to move forward more confidently. A spread can also help you make more conscious decisions if the path forward is not clear.

We all have life patterns that sometimes hold us back or sabotage our efforts to grow and move forward in life. A multi-card spread can help identify those patterns and offer guidance around your thought processes.

A multi-card spread can also give you more nuanced guidance for a period of time, like a lunar cycle. This allows you to work with the cycle's energies to align better with timing and manage your own energy.

SETTING UP & INTERPRETING SPREADS

Put yourself in a peaceful, receptive space, using whatever tools feel supportive for the work ahead. Reverentially hold your deck and close your eyes. Either meditate or say a few words of prayer or affirmation so that you tune in to the energy of the cards and the querent.

After asking what questions should be addressed, lay out the spread, shuffling and taking your time as you do. Trust your knowing as to whether you shuffle between each card or not. Energetically tune in to which card is next to be pulled. Sometimes the cards jump out, so trust that if they do.

Take an overview first. To do this, look at the suit elements and the overall makeup or whether it's primarily made up of cards from the Major or Minor Arcana. Look at the planetary, sign, and house connections as a whole alongside the numbers and any other symbols that speak to you.

Then begin giving your reading. Provide an overview of the elemental themes and then speak to each card as you feel is needed. Look at how each card leads into the next as part of the story the cards are weaving. Over time, the story will become more fluid, allowing you to provide guidance from your intuition rather from learned knowledge. Most important, relax and enjoy your relationship with the cards.

Next, let's look at some sample spreads.

FIVE SAMPLES & READINGS

In the following five sample spreads, you will find some ideas for spreads. There are countless others, along with interpretation methods. Again, remember that everything in this book is a suggestion to get you started, not rigid rules that can't be broken.

CREATING YOUR OWN SPREADS

The five sample spreads shown are a small representation of tarot spreads. In fact, the possibilities are endless, and I once more encourage you to explore what works for you. Create your own spreads by following your intuition.

As you learn to read the Tarot through the lens of astrology, you might want to create a spread based on a querent's natal chart or a major transit they are experiencing. A **transit** is when the current position of a planet aspects (or creates an angle in) the querent's natal chart. An example of this might be transiting Neptune square in the querent's twelfth house, Sagittarius Sun. Of course, this understanding will come over time.

I invite you to ask the cards what spread might help the querent most as you develop your relationship with the cards. Ask the question while holding the cards and tuning in to the querent. Trust what you get. Because the potential for different spreads is endless, there is no right way to do this.

FULL MOON FIVE-CARD SPREAD

The intent of this spread is to offer guidance. Pull a card for the sign the full moon is in as the significator (the card that represents the querent), and then pull the next four cards to represent what needs attention, expansion, and energy focus, as well as the overall purpose of this lunar cycle.

CARDS IN THE SPREAD

1. Querent (center)

2. Attention (middle row, left)

3. Expansion (middle row, right)

4. Energy focus (top)

5. Overall purpose (bottom)

A full moon spread is designed to ask for guidance for the coming month until the next full moon. Its purpose is to connect with the energy of the full moon and ask what the universe wants you to know using the Major Arcana card corresponding with the sign of the full moon as the querent or significator, in this case the Star/Aquarius card.

First look at the overall elements. This is an air full moon, and the cards bring fire (the wands) in positions two and three, suggesting that there's a lot of creative and spiritual mental focus and inspiration to expand upon, because fire and air work to fan the flames of self-expression. The only earth element is the six of pentacles in position four, suggesting that you must focus your energy on bringing the inspiration and creativity down to earth and sharing the wealth. The overall purpose of the lunar month is also air, as Knights are considered to be air cards and, if you look at the Knight in the card, it suggests motivated, forward-thinking action.

Consider numbers and modalities. In position two, we have an eight, the number of mastery. The mutable modality suggests mastering change. Position three is a two, the number of balance and the cardinal modality of new projects, asking you to focus on what you are moving toward. Position four brings a six and the fixed modality, asking you to ground this wild energy of fire and air to achieve your goals.

6 OF PENTACLES

8 OF WANDS

THE STAR

2 OF WANDS

KNIGHT OF SWORDS

THREE-CARD SPREAD

The three-card spread is useful for so many questions and provides quick guidance around a situation or question, the obstacles or focus needed, and the potential outcome if the cards' guidance is heeded.

CARDS IN THE SPREAD

1. Situation (left)

2. Action (middle)

3. Outcome (right)

For this sample, I asked the question "Should I take the new job I have been offered?" A three-card spread gives very clear guidance for this type of question.

Approach this spread card by card rather than through an elemental overview.

The World card corresponds to Saturn, the planet of mastery, maturity, and achievement, which suggests a cycle has completed and a new one is beginning. Card 2 is pure inspirational fire and new beginnings. The outcome is a mix of water (the Queen) and air (swords), suggesting that having the courage and desire to take the action of beginning the new role will bring both mental and emotional fulfilment. Quite simply, the cards answer that yes, you are ready for the new job.

THE WORLD

ACE OF WANDS

QUEEN OF SWORDS

FIVE-CARD SPREAD

Another simple spread to answer a more specific question is a five-card spread that adds a little more nuance than the three-card spread, resulting in more detailed guidance.

CARDS IN THE SPREAD

1. Querent (top vertical)

2. Challenge (top horizontal)

3. Advice (second row left)

4. Advice (second row middle)

5. Advice (second row right)

For this spread, I asked the question "Should I leave my relationship?" When relationships are concerned, the cards are speaking to the internal feelings of the querent. Be cautious when giving your advice, and ask questions for clarity.

Allow the overall message to speak to you after looking at the card representing the querent, the ace of wands, which suggests that the querent is ready for a new start and to take action. The other four cards suggest mental and emotional stress (the swords and cups) and the need for major change through action (the Tower). The challenge card,

covering the card representing the querent, is the seven of swords, suggesting that the challenge may be deception of some kind. Because the card relates to the querent, the deception may be the querent not being truthful with themselves.

The advice cards indicate the need to come to terms with emotional disappointment, perhaps that the relationship isn't fulfilling the querent's emotional needs. The Knight of swords would ask you to advise the querent to gain some clarity on the challenge—to journal or perhaps talk through their mental challenge—before moving forward. The Tower card indicates that the relationship either needs a fresh start in some way or to end and for the person to move on. The Tower is the Mars card, and Mars is connected to the card representing the querent. Mars is action and passion, so yes, it's time to gain mental clarity around desires and move forward.

7 OF SWORDS

ACE OF WANDS

5 OF CUPS

KNIGHT OF SWORDS

THE TOWER

12-SIGN SPREAD

The most commonly used tarot astrology spread is the 13-card, 12-sign spread, with the center, 13th card, as the outcome. These spreads are useful for in-depth guidance in more complex situations and provide guidance for about six months ahead. Pull the cards and lay them out in the order given below using the keywords that come to your mind as you pull each card. You are asking the cards to show you the answer at each stage. I asked for general guidance in this reading.

CARDS IN THE SPREAD

1. Aries: The individual (12 o'clock)

2. Taurus: Material, self-worth (1 o'clock)

3. Gemini: Communication (2 o'clock)

4. Cancer: Home, family (3 o'clock)

5. Leo: Creativity, heart (4 o'clock)

6. Virgo. Work, health (5 o'clock)

7. Libra: Significant relationships (6 o'clock)

8. Scorpio: Transformation (7 o'clock)

9. Sagittarius: Higher learning, travel (8 o'clock)

10. Capricorn: Public status (9 o'clock)

11. Aquarius: Groups (10 o'clock)

12. Pisces: Dreams, mysticism (11 o'clock)

13. Outcome (center)

To read this spread, combine the meaning of the card and the sign as you move around the wheel of life. Take the first sign, Aries at 12 o'clock, as the individual. The five of wands suggests conflicting passions—an internal identity conflict. Look at it as a path of influence over the next few months. As you move through each card, you can offer guidance about the internal strife that dominates this card and reflect on where the querent can find support. For example, the Sun in the area of relationships suggests that will be an area that the querent can lean into.

The card at twelve o'clock suggests internal conflict on what action to take. The card at one o'clock suggests a test of faith around that conflict. The card at two o'clock suggests the querent might be missing some information by not asking open questions. The card at three o'clock suggests the need to go within to get clarity. The card at four o'clock invites the querent to reflect on their past to find creative inspiration. The card at five o'clock asks what kind of work will bring emotional fulfilment. The card at six o'clock suggests finding support from your significant relationships. The card at seven o'clock suggests deep internal transformation or shadow work. The card at eight o'clock suggests that higher learning or a change of belief of some kind may bring emotional fulfillment. The card at nine o'clock suggests mental anguish, perhaps from worrying what the world thinks. The card at ten o'clock indicates the querent's creative leadership qualities to a group or groups. The card at 11 o'clock indicates tuning in to mystical states to access their dreams. Card 13, in the center, represents the outcome, as in the overall message of the cards, and that suggests that the querent's own limiting beliefs are a holdup.

4 OF CUPS

9 OF WANDS

5 OF WANDS

TEMPERANCE

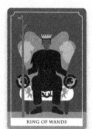

KING OF WANDS

2 OF WANDS

8 OF SWORDS

9 OF SWORDS

6 OF CUPS

THE HIGH PRIESTESS

THE SUN

JUDGMENT

9 OF CUPS

HORSESHOE SPREAD

As you develop your tarot practice, you can move on to playing with spreads of different shapes. One of those is the horseshoe spread, which is very useful for major decision-making. There are different meanings assigned to the seven cards in this spread, and you can assign your own, but the suggested meanings in this instance are provided below. Please tune in to each meaning as you pull each card. This spread can also be laid out as a reversed horseshoe. Again, tune in to the energy of each meaning as you pull each card.

CARDS IN THE SPREAD

1. Past influences

2. Present issue

3. Future developments

4. Advice for the querent

5. How people around the issue affect the querent's decision

6. Obstacles or hidden influences

7. Optimal action for resolution

For this reading, I asked the question "I have been offered a long-distance move in my career, which means moving my family. Should I accept?"

Look at the overall elements and whether there are Major Arcana cards, suggesting big life changes. Elementally, the Minor Arcana are all fire and earth, suggesting inspiration, action, and material changes. The two Major Arcana are both water cards (Death is Scorpio and the High Priestess is the Moon), suggesting that there's a lot of emotional transformation connected to this move.

Looking at the individual cards, the past influences (six of wands) suggest that a peak of success has been reached up to now. Death represents the present issue, suggesting that this is a big upheaval and a complete life transformation. Future development comes from the three of wands, which represents travel and forward movement. The ace of pentacles is in the advice position, suggesting a new beginning materially. The eight of wands suggests that people around the querent think they should undertake this move and that a quick decision is in order. The obstacles or hidden influences come through the six of pentacles, suggesting that the querent is trying to balance the needs of everyone involved. Lastly, the High Priestess in the last position suggests that the querent is being

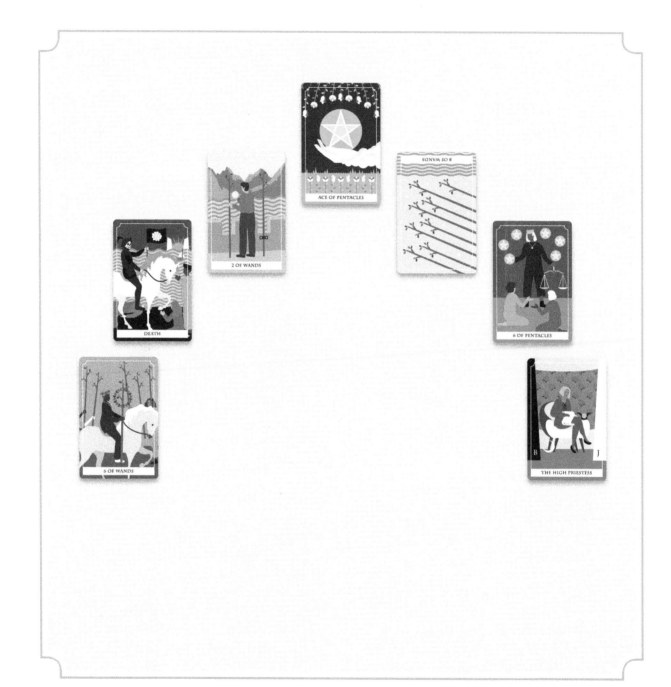

asked to trust themselves. Because the overall reading is a positive one, if the querent's intuitive pull is to say yes, then that's the best move.

CONCLUSION

The world of tarot and astrology will now start to become your oyster as you practice with different spreads and start to create your own. As always, the key is to keep practicing.

Try out different spreads, and each time, look at the astrological symbolism from a bird's-eye view and in each card. Over time, you will see more and more in the cards. I still have days where I wonder how I didn't see something before. Remember to look at the elements, the Major and Minor Arcana, the court cards, the suits, the numbers, and the decans, bringing in the connected astrological meanings at all times until it becomes second nature.

II

UNVEILING
THE CARDS

Part II will uncover more detailed information about each of the 78 cards in the tarot deck within the context of astrology. Each chapter will walk you through the cards in the Major and Minor Arcana, their associated planets and signs, the meaning of images and symbols, upright and reverse keywords, and how to better understand their significance in readings.

6

THE MAJOR ARCANA: THE FOOL THROUGH THE WORLD

In this chapter, you are going to take a deeper look at each of the Major Arcana cards and how to interpret them through the lens of astrology. The Major Arcana cards represent bigger life issues and also archetypal lessons. The cards follow the journey of growth known as the Fool's (or Hero's) journey and are usually seen as a linear or cyclical path of development. Understanding the astrological connections will help you connect the cards to archetypal growth. Let's look at each one individually.

0: THE FOOL

THE FOOL

Planet/sign: Uranus

Element: Air

Numerology: 0: alpha and omega

Colors: Blue-green

Symbols: Youth, dog, mountains, and a cliff edge

Upright keywords: Spontaneity, originality, eccentricity, uniqueness, personal freedom, potential, and fearlessness

Reversed keywords: Gullibility, blocks, recklessness, naivety, no sense of adventure, and lack of direction

In astrology, Uranus represents light-bulb innovation, sudden change, and excitement, but also recklessness and willfulness. Reading the Fool card through the energy of Uranus and the element of air, we can see it as the energy of sudden mental inspiration that starts the Fool on a new journey. The card shows an eager youth skipping along with a playful dog, and it looks as if the youth may be about to leave solid ground and fall or fly off a cliff's edge. The 0 is the energy of unlimited potential. The energy of Uranus is that of lightning strikes, suggesting an unexpected new journey.

In love or relationships, this can represent taking the chance on a new relationship or thinking differently about relationships. It can also represent the journey of leaving a relationship, depending on the question. The excitement of a new start is here, but also the caution against recklessness and lack of thought if the card is reversed.

If the question is about career and wealth, the Fool card and Uranus usually suggest sudden and unexpected opportunities if it is upright, as well as remaining open to possibilities that have not been previously considered.

If the focus of the reading is success and happiness, have a short conversation with the querent to understand how they define those things. If the focus is overall success and happiness in all areas, the Fool suggests exciting spiritual revelations and a feeling of awakening to possibilities, along with a sense of optimism and excitement about the future.

As a wild card, the placement of the card in the spread would help you read its meaning. But primarily, the card—like Uranus—means sudden insights or change, and is an invitation to remain open to all possibilities.

I: THE MAGICIAN

THE MAGICIAN

Planet/sign: Mercury

Element: Air

Numerology: 1: new beginnings

Colors: Red, and blue

Symbols: All four elements, red rose, double-tipped wand, infinity symbol, stars, right arm raised to spirit, and left arm pointing down to earth

Upright keywords: Magic, creation, juggling, skill, resources, and intention

Reversed keywords: Manipulation, trickery, and lack of knowledge or listening skills

Mercury is the messenger of the gods, moving between the gods and humans and bringing the language of source down to Earth. Mercury also represents trickster energy and the ability to integrate complex ideas and information. This planet also represents alchemy, a process of transformation or chemistry. All of this is reflected in the Magician card, with all the elements being juggled to create infinite potential. The red rose represents passion, and the stars and the position of the arms suggest the ability to create by combining what is above and below to make your ideas manifest. The double-tipped wand is the tool of the Magician, who often says "abracadabra," meaning "I create as I speak" (Mercury is speech).

In readings about love and relationship, this card can be read as a need for communication or being open to new ideas and making desires manifest. Reversed, it can mean having a rethink in a current relationship.

In career and wealth, this is also a card of intention—of using mental skills and resources to conjure up a promotion, a new job, or something to increase the querent's wealth. If it appears reversed, it suggests blocking your own resources.

Similarly, for goals and core values, this represents the ability to manifest desires. Offer guidance around limiting beliefs, especially if the card is reversed, or suggest tools that can help the querent get clear on their desires and how to create the success and happiness for which they long.

When this card is a wild card, it should be read in light of the other cards in the spread to show where the querent is blocked from creating magic in their lives. Remind them they have everything they need to do so.

THE HIGH PRIESTESS

II: THE HIGH PRIESTESS

The Moon corresponds to the High Priestess card and represents our inner life, intuition, and feelings. The Moon has night energy and guides our way in the dark when the veil between the worlds is thin and the duality of the stark energy of day is more diffuse. The Moon is ancient knowledge—the intuitive, feeling self. This understanding can help you tune in to the energy of the High Priestess and connect with inner, ancient wisdom. The symbolism on the card takes us back to the Songs of Solomon, the roses of passion, and the veil, to the contrast between the rational day energy and feeling night energy.

If the reading is focused on love and relationships, this is a clear message to trust your intuition. The presence of this card could indicate doubts or even blocks that are keeping you from finding love. If reversed, it suggests that you may be trusting gossip or attempting to rationalize rather than going with your inner wisdom.

In career or wealth matters, this can represent uncertainty and doubt—a feeling of not being sure which direction you are going in or what's happening in these areas. If reversed, this is even more challenging and represents strong resistance to self-trust.

The High Priestess also suggests a lack of clarity around goals and values—a feeling of aimlessness—and is always a call to learn to tune in to the subconscious, which is not always easy. When reversed, the resistance is greater.

The High Priestess as a wild card is always going to indicate listening to your inner voice and/or spiritual consciousness, whether that be through meditation, journaling, walking in nature, or using one of countless other tools.

Planet/sign: The Moon

Element: Water

Numerology: 2: balance

Colors: Red, blue or green, black, and white

Symbols: Pillars of Solomon's Temple (Boaz/strength, Jachin/establishment, black/white duality), and ancient scroll

Upright keywords: Inner wisdom, ancient knowledge, spirituality, subconscious, and divine yin/feminine

Reversed keywords: Lack of self-trust, disconnectedness from emotions/spirituality, and needing alone time/meditation

III: THE EMPRESS

THE EMPRESS

Planet/sign: Venus

Element: Earth

Numerology: 3: creation

Colors: Blue or green, red, and yellow

Symbols: Throne, scepter, grain, and crown

Upright keywords: Mother archetype, mother nature, creativity, nurturing, sensuality, and passion

Reversed keywords: Lack of love, feeling unnurtured/ unloved, and blocked creativity

Venus is a complex energy and is said to represent the higher energy of Earth, and that is how she is represented in the Empress card. This is Gaia, the Earth Mother who is fertile, nurturing, and abundant. As ruler of Libra (air) and Taurus (earth), Venus is in her earthly energy in this card. She is sensual, connected to all that you can see, hear, touch, smell, and taste, representing connection with the Earth and nurturing. The Empress has a passionate connection with life and nature and is a call to make self-love and love of others a priority. The Empress also represents creative endeavors.

In a reading where a querent asks about love and relationships, the Empress could be a call to embody the energy of love in self-care or a call for working toward healthier relationships with others. Reversed, this card generally leads to guidance around making self-care a priority.

For questions related to career and wealth, this card is a great sign, as Venus also represents a growth in abundance. Career-wise, it could indicate a pay raise or promotion, or pursuing a career in a creative field. Reversed, this card generally means that there are blocks to this abundance.

The Empress is also a great card for questions about goals and values, as Venus also represents core values. In this case, the card could be suggesting that love should be brought to the front and center as a core value.

When the Empress is a wild card, it can represent a supportive, loving, and motherly presence in the querent's life, or the querent embodying these qualities, dependent on where it shows up in a reading. Remember, this is archetypal, so speak to bigger, ongoing, themes.

IV: THE EMPEROR

THE EMPEROR

Planet/sign: Aries

Element: Fire

Numerology: 4: foundation

Colors: Red

Symbols: Throne, mountains, orb, ankh scepter, and crown

Upright keywords: Structure, stability, father archetype, power, and leadership

Reversed keywords: Lacking or abusing power, controlling, and authoritarianism

Aries, ruled by Mars and a cardinal sign, is a sign of leadership, self-assertion, and action. Aries is very sure of itself, has a strong will, and is very enterprising, incisive, and passionate. Because Aries is so sure and focused, it builds solid and stable foundations. However, Aries can also be controlling and bullying if the shadow traits are represented.

The Emperor card has symbols that also represent stable leadership. The ankh scepter represents life force itself, the orb represents divine power, the throne represents power, and the mountains represent stability.

In love and relationships, this card can either represent a need for the querent to step into a courageous space or to be more dominant in going after what they desire. It can also represent seeking the advice of a father figure or even the appearance of a fatherly figure in romance. Aries also represents clarity of purpose and incisiveness, so the reading may be asking for the querent to get very clear on something.

If the query is about career and wealth, this is likely a call to leadership or to begin a new role that has more of a leadership element. It can also mean a strong leader figure appearing in the querent's life.

If the Emperor card appears in a question about goals and values, this is a call for someone to create strong and stable goals, to get very clear on what those goals are, and to step into their personal power.

If the Emperor is a wild card, it often represents a father archetype appearing where it's needed, though it may also speak to embodying the archetype within.

V: THE HIEROPHANT

THE HIEROPHANT

Planet/sign: Taurus

Element: Earth

Numerology: 5: change

Colors: Red, orange, and yellow

Symbols: Spiritual teacher, keys, staff, benediction crown, and student

Upright keywords: Teacher, higher knowledge, belief systems, traditions, priest, and spiritual wisdom

Reversed keywords: Dogma, unethical teacher/teaching, and challenging tradition

The Hierophant's connection to Taurus reflects the grounded, fixed energy of the card. And yet, the card is numbered five, which is the number of change and communication. Taurus is a solid, materialistic sign. Combining all the symbolism suggests teaching and learning about the practical, material application of spiritual teachings on Earth. In ancient Greece, the Hierophant was the priest/ess figure, specifically connected to the Eleusinian mysteries, through which people were taught to find direct experience of the divine, and the priest/ess was more of an interpreter of spiritual wisdom. This is about connecting to our earthly incarnation grounded in solid spiritual principles.

The Hierophant is the Taurus card and has a fixed, earthly energy. In love and relationship readings, this card suggests physicality, sensuality, and material issues. If the card is upright, it might be a call to a more sensual enjoyment within the relationship, or a teacher of some kind guiding the relationship.

In career and wealth, there's a call to ground the material and work life in solid values and more traditional wisdom. Taurus wants solidity, so advice around making financial or career matters more solid is required.

Taurus is ruled by Venus, which represents core values. So, when the Hierophant appears in a reading around goals and values, it's a call to get clear about those core values so that goals come from a grounded place.

As a wild card, this could mean the need to seek higher knowledge or the advice of a wise teacher, or to step into a teacher/guide role. It's also a call to explore beliefs in a deeper way and to become more grounded in those beliefs.

VI: THE LOVERS

The Lovers card is represented by the sign of Gemini, which is about so much more than the love between a couple. Gemini is the sign of the twins and is ruled by Mercury, the planet that connects the realm of the gods and that of humanity. This card is more about the union of all polarities rather than lovers, though it may apply to that also. As an air sign, Gemini represents ideas and connection of the mind and ideas, so this card is more about harmony and union of all opposites, including through inner alignment, community, and self-love.

In the context of love and relationships, this card is more likely to represent love in a one-on-one relationship and is generally a wonderful omen for an existing relationship. It can also mean a decision about a relationship issue is due.

When a querent asks about career and wealth, this card may suggest connecting with a community mindset or choices around job options and the need for communication. It can also indicate a partnership of a financial nature.

For readings about goals and values, the Lovers card can suggest a relationship and community-focused approach to setting goals and to getting clear on core values. It could be an opportunity to suggest getting clear on what a querent's values are in relationships and to base their goals around that.

As a wild card, the Lovers card represents choices and decisions around community and relationships. Where does the querent need to find more connection and to listen to different points of view?

THE LOVERS

Planet/sign: Gemini

Element: Air

Numerology: 6: harmony

Colors: Green, red, yellow, and white

Symbols: Man, woman, black, white, angel/cupid, tree of knowledge, heaven, and earth

Upright keywords: Love, community, union of polarities, choices, and friendship

Reversed keywords: Feeling unsure, disconnectedness, polarization, and lack of community

VII: THE CHARIOT

THE CHARIOT

Planet/sign: Cancer

Element: Water

Numerology: 7: reflection

Colors: Blue, black, and white

Symbols: Chariot, armored warrior, lingam and yoni symbol (the encircled rod on the winged shield), and black-and-white sphinxes/lions/horses

Upright keywords: Discipline, centered control, preparedness, focus, and momentum

Reversed keywords: Rushing, lack of discipline, lack of preparedness, and lack of control

Cancer is the sign of the Moon, and the symbol is the two Cancer pincers that close in together to protect the crab in the shell. It's a sign of inner strength and tenaciousness that protects and nurtures the inner life, family, and home. This is reflected in the Chariot card as the armed warrior in their chariot (home), gathering the opposing forces within (black-and-white sphinxes/lions to unite the lingam and yoni, which represent the inseparable male and female, the passive and active polarities from which all life originates). The Chariot represents forward movement but is not actually yet moving, so it is more about a gathering of opposites before gaining forward momentum.

In a love and relationship reading, the Chariot is about coming together in preparedness for aligned momentum and forward movement. This could literally mean a marriage or creating a family, or a renewed focus on coming together so that you can move forward in aligned action. "Stronger together" might be a good term to use.

If the Chariot is drawn in a career and wealth reading, the card's interpretation may be more about inner resilience and momentum. This would suggest applying inner focus to the issue at hand.

In a goals and values reading, the Chariot suggests a strong inner focus to get emotional clarity on values and to create focused goals rather than moving forward without a clear focus.

As a wild card, the Chariot always represents where an area of focus and a gathering of inner emotional strength is advised before moving forward.

VIII: STRENGTH

STRENGTH

Planet/sign: Leo

Element: Fire

Numerology: 8: mastery

Colors: Orange, green, and white

Symbols: Lion, woman, infinity/strength symbol, and trees/mountains

Upright keywords: Courage, taming chaos, inner strength, solidity, and compassion

Reversed keywords: Fear, compulsion, allowing chaos to guide, lack of grounding, and self-doubt

Leo, a fixed fire sign, is associated with the Strength card in the Tarot, and in astrology, Leo rules the heart. The word "courage" comes from *cœur*, the French word for "heart." This symbology reveals the meaning of this card as finding true strength from finding inner balance. The numeral eight turned on its side is the infinity symbol. Connection with the infinite comes from grounding. The imagery of the trees or mountains in the heart reflect this. The image of the woman calming the lion suggests calming inner fiery compulsions and outer chaos, potentially advising tapping into inner confidence and strength.

If the Strength card appears in a love and relationship reading, you are being asked to follow your heart's desire and to lead with the heart. It can also mean finding the courage to be compassionate and to show your heart.

In a career or wealth reading, the Strength card can mean finding the courage to create what your heart really wants. Leo is a creative sign, so this might mean having the courage to follow your creative impulses.

If values and goals are the focus of the reading, this card is a call for courageous and strong goals based on what brings joy (as Leo also rules joy).

If the Strength card is a wild card, it calls for courage and confidence in the querent's inner strength while also exercising compassion for the self.

IX: THE HERMIT

THE HERMIT

Planet/sign: Virgo

Element: Earth

Numerology: 9: accomplishment

Colors: Earth colors, brown, and green

Symbols: Mountains, lamp, staff, cloak, and sky

Upright keywords: Wisdom, spiritual mastery, solitude, and self-reflection

Reversed keywords: Needing solitude, too much solitude and navel gazing, and anti-social perspective

Virgo is a sign of usefulness, deeper meaning, practicality, purity, and perfectionism. Virgo is also a sign that means becoming whole unto oneself. All of this is represented in the Hermit card. Hermits are loners, focused on their inner, spiritual enlightenment and growth. Both Virgo and the Hermit are introspective and analytical, and this can mean both personal analysis or seeking the guidance of a wise counselor or guide. The mountains represent development and success but also a sense of being alone on the mountaintop.

In a love and relationship reading, this card can suggest that some deep soul-searching is necessary to be in a healthy relationship. As the analysis card, it calls for introspection and alone time before strong relationships can be forged.

If the Hermit is pulled in a reading related to career and wealth, it might suggest that either career or monetary success are not spiritually fulfilling the querent and that some soul-searching around what really holds meaning for the person is necessary.

In a reading related to values and goals, the Hermit card is a clear message that some time alone to find what has deep meaning is required. The lamp represents the light of inner knowing illuminating the way forward.

As a wild card, the Hermit always calls for a period of self-refection, though its meaning can be influenced by the other cards in the reading.

X: THE WHEEL OF FORTUNE

WHEEL OF FORTUNE

Planet/sign: Jupiter

Element: All four elements

Numerology: 10: new beginnings and completion

Colors: Blue, white, orange, brown, and black

Symbols: Wheel, clouds, constellations, sphinx, snake, and Anubis

Upright keywords: Change, wheel of life, endings/beginnings, and fortune

Reversed keywords: Stagnation, lack of progress, setbacks, and warning to slow down

Jupiter is the planet of expansion, fortune, aspiration, and freedom. It is also the planet associated with the Wheel of Fortune card. Astrology works in twelves—12 signs, 12 houses, 12 months of the year, and Jupiter's 12-year cycle. Jupiter is often associated with periods of expansion and growth for the individual. Understanding both the energy of Jupiter the 12-year cycle helps in the interpretation of this card.

The Wheel of Fortune indicates change—endings and beginnings. In life, change of some kind is inevitable, and fortunes are cyclical, involving all the elements. This is represented in the Wheel of Fortune or the sacred hoop, with the primary corresponding element being fire, which is the energy of the phoenix rising from the ashes.

If the Wheel of Fortune appears in a love and relationship reading, it indicates a new relationship or newly energized relationship. Relationships often go through cycles, and this suggests a feeling of expansiveness and freedom in those areas. It can also mean the ending of an unhealthy relationship.

In a career and wealth reading, this card is a wonderful omen for increased fortunes—perhaps as the result of a new job—and improved luck in financial matters

As a wild card, the Wheel of Fortune represents change and expanded fortunes, and it should be read in conjunction with the other cards in the spread to ascertain where that change might come.

XI: JUSTICE

JUSTICE

Planet/sign: Libra

Element: Air

Numerology: 11: balance

Colors: Purple, black, and white

Symbols: Scales, sword, pillars, and crown

Upright keywords: Accountability, justice, fairness, and balance

Reversed keywords: Unfairness, dishonesty, and lack of balance

Libra is associated with justice and the scales of diplomacy, weighing up options, and mediation. This is a great way to begin to understand the Justice card. As an air sign, Libra is about mental balance and listening to other viewpoints to come to agreements. That could relate to people with differing perspectives or internal struggles. The scales of justice are also about accountability, as Libra is a sign of relationship and community. So, if actions are causing harm to others, the Justice card often appears, suggesting that consequences are coming. This card and sign can also speak to legal or court proceedings.

In love and relationships, the Justice card suggests that harmony can only be found by listening to the other person and meeting each other halfway. If reversed, this card may point to dishonesty, unfairness, or lack of listening skills.

If career and wealth is the focus of the reading, the Justice card can suggest an imbalance in the workplace, a legal matter, or a need for mediation and diplomacy.

If the Justice card is pulled for a query around values and goals, it's a call to find balance when creating those goals and to balance seemingly conflicting core values.

As a wild card, Justice might suggest that there are some repercussions for actions taken that have led to an imbalance or unfairness.

XII: THE HANGED MAN

THE HANGED MAN

Planet/sign: Neptune

Element: Water

Numerology: 12/3: creation

Colors: Green or blue and red

Symbols: Tree, man, noose, crossed leg, and illuminated head

Upright keywords: Letting go, perception, perspective, waiting, enlightenment, and trust

Reversed keywords: Victimhood, procrastination, stagnation, and disconnection from source

Neptune is the planet of oneness, mysticism, transcendence, escapism, and inspiration. It's the most nebulous of energies, and, as a water sign with night and yin energy, it connects us emotionally to source, spirit, god, or whatever the divine is for you. Neptune is also a dissolving energy that can be confusing to the rational, linear world.

When the Hanged Man is pulled in a reading, a great phrase to use can be "Let go and let god," indicating a need to slow down and wait for answers to come. Perspectives are not often changed by overthinking, and this card invites the querent to relax and wait a while. The illuminated head is at the bottom and the male (usually representing active, linear energy) figure is completely relaxed and upside down, suggesting the need to let go of that energy for a while.

In a love and relationship reading, the Hanged Man suggests a lack of trust and perhaps even controlling tendencies. It is a call to just slow down, let go of the need to control things, and allow other perspectives in.

If the reading is about career and wealth issues, the Hanged Man suggests a pause to allow clarity to come.

In a reading that is focused on values and goals, this card is likely to suggest turning to spiritual pursuits to gain clarity, perhaps through meditation or a new spiritual path. It could also be saying that lack of spiritual clarity is the issue at hand.

As a wild card, the Hanged Man always suggests a slowdown or a pause, as taking time to trust that things will unfold in their own time without the need to push can result in the best outcomes.

XIII: DEATH

DEATH

Planet/sign: Scorpio

Element: Water

Numerology: 13¾: foundation

Colors: Black, white, blue, and gold

Symbols: Grim Reaper skeleton wearing black armor, white horse, banner with white rose, dead body, water with sailing boat, and rising or setting sun between pillars

Upright keywords: Transformation, death and rebirth, regeneration, and endings/beginnings

Reversed keywords: Fear of change and burning bridges

One of the most feared cards in the Tarot is the Death card. It is associated with one of the most maligned of signs, Scorpio, the deepest of water signs. There's a probing intensity to Scorpio, as this is a sign that dives into the darkest shadows of the psyche, where all that is taboo is often hidden. Scorpio is also a fixed sign, so it's more about stability than change. That's what makes the Death card one that often challenges people, as it brings up fear of change, fear of transformation, and fear of actual death, all of which are inevitable at some point.

In a reading regarding love and relationships, this card can indicate major transformation, such as the end of a relationship and a fresh start. It can also mean changing and transforming how the person relates in relationships so that strong, new foundations are laid.

If the reading is about career and wealth, then the Death card can, of course, mean a great change in circumstances is coming, such as in career of finances. However, look to the psychological depth of Scorpio for the potential to create strong foundations based on deepest desires, releasing things that no longer support the querent, for a stronger reading.

The Death card in a reading about values and goals is a call for some deep soul-searching to get in touch with deeply held values. Ask the querent what really has meaning for them, what feels meaningless at this stage in their life? Personal values and goals can change over time, and this card suggests that the client is ready for deeper meaning in their life.

As a wild card, the Death card always comes at a point of change, asking what needs to end and what's beginning.

XIV: TEMPERANCE

TEMPERANCE

Planet/sign: Sagittarius

Element: Fire

Numerology: $^{14}/_5$: change

Colors: Gold, blue, white, and green

Symbols: Winged angel, one foot on earth, one in water, two cups pouring water/spirit, and the Sun

Upright keywords: Compromise, patience, moderation, higher vision, and peace

Reversed keywords: Dogmatic views and uncompromising attitudes

The association of the Temperance card with Sagittarius, a fire sign, is an unusual one, as this mutable sign can be rather rash and dogmatic at times. However, that connects us more to the reverse meaning of the card. The energy of Sagittarius is a striving for a higher vision and knowledge, which usually means finding the wisdom of the middle way, or "tempering" more extreme energies by combining the oppositional impulses. The pouring of liquid/spirit from one cup to another is a form of balancing, and so is the symbolism of one foot on the ground and one in water. The angel itself represents an enlightened state of being. This card is a call to temper the extremes by exercising patience and moderation.

In a love and relationship reading, the Temperance card can suggest that the querent is being forceful and pushy in this area, or that the person is being too reserved. This card is always a call for balancing extremes and exercising moderation.

If the Temperance card comes up in a career and wealth reading, it's a call for balance and moderation. It can also mean that rewards are coming in through a temperate and balanced approach.

If a query is about goals and values, the Temperance card can mean that the querent is either being overly cautious or rigid, or that their aspirations are over the top. Try to find the middle way by getting clear on core values and tempering goals with a mix of realism and aspirational thinking.

When Temperance is pulled as a wild card, it's always a sign to practice moderation and patience in whatever area of life the reading speaks to.

XV: THE DEVIL

THE DEVIL

Planet/sign: Capricorn

Element: Earth

Numerology: $^{15}/_{6}$: harmony

Colors: Brown, black, and gray

Symbols: Horned goat/devil, inverted pentagram, and naked male/female chained figures

Upright keywords: Restrictions, addictions, fears, shadow, and limiting beliefs

Reversed keywords: Overcoming limiting beliefs, breaking free, finishing jobs, and relationships

Capricorn is an interesting sign that mellows with age. Fearful, serious, and full of traits that "bedevil" in youth, this sign becomes less conservative, less somber, and lighter with age. Like the sign, the Devil card is somewhat reversed. The upright reading suggests blocks, limiting beliefs, restrictions, and sometimes addictions, which are often there to fill a void created by fears. A reversed Devil suggests that the querent is breaking free of those bedevilments and leaving behind old habits and patterns that have held them back. As this is the Capricorn card and the older, wiser Capricorn has a sensual, dry humor, it can be helpful to ask them to take a kind, light-hearted approach with their fears and ask if they are real or false.

If the Devil card comes up in a love and relationship reading, this often represents the querent's own fears of not being enough for their partner or for a healthy relationship, because fear is a big shadow for the Capricorn.

In a career and wealth reading, the Devil card can again represent the querent's fears of not being good enough, of success, and of failure. The client may believe they always do things a certain way or will never be successful, but such limiting beliefs are just that.

The Devil card is a great card to get in a reading focused on goals and values because Capricorn is an ambitious energy. Focusing on achievement and diligence while overcoming that shadow of fear is useful.

As a wild card, the Devil is always pointing to those fears and limiting beliefs holding people back.

XVI: THE TOWER

THE TOWER

Planet/sign: Mars

Element: Fire

Numerology: $^{16}/_7$: reflection

Colors: Black, white, blue, and orange

Symbols: Tower, fire, falling people, and thunderstorm

Upright keywords: Shock, chaos, devastation and regeneration, and revelation

Reversed keywords: Resistance to change, ongoing chaos, shaking the table, and mental breakdown

The Tower is another card that elicits fear in most people when it shows up in a reading. Like Mars, the planet associated with the card, it's not always the easiest of energies, as the change heralded by Mars and the Tower can be sudden and aggressive. However, deeper meanings are represented here. Chaos and change are a part of life, and sometimes change comes quickly. This card topples shaky foundations, and Mars likes fast action. Mars is, however, a protector, a guard, and a warrior. If foundations are not solid, they often need rebuilding, so think of this card as the breakdown before a breakthrough, leading to rebuilding something more lasting.

In a love or relationship reading, the Tower can suggest a breakdown of an unhealthy relationship. It can also suggest major breakthroughs within the querent or relationship to make a solid relationship more possible. Always be mindful of the possibilities of rebuilding contained within the card.

In a career and wealth reading, this card can suggest a big shakeup in either of those areas. But then again, it can also suggest that the querent might have some revelations about situations that are not built on solid foundations so they can shake things up for themselves. Sometimes, we have to shake tables to achieve what we desire.

If the Tower is pulled around goals and values, the message is to get clear on core values and to let go of anything that isn't aligned with those values. That means that goals can be created to build something much more aligned with the querent's values.

If the Tower is pulled as a wild card, caution the querent that some kind of chaos is likely. Emphasize that out of chaos, a more solid foundation can be built.

XVII: THE STAR

THE STAR

Planet/sign: Aquarius

Element: Air

Numerology: $^{17}/_8$: mastery

Colors: Blue, gold, and white

Symbols: Figure, pouring spirit from jugs, stars, water, bird, and land

Upright keywords: Inspiration, renewal, downloads, positivity, and peace

Reversed keywords: Negativity, hopelessness, pessimism, and ignoring messages from the cosmos

Aquarius and the Star are both about making sense of the bigger picture—what we find when we connect to our higher, intuitive mind, intellect, and consciousness, and ground it in inventive and unique ideas on Earth. Aquarius is associated with astrology, allowing this card to bring messages from the stars down to Earth. The sign of Aquarius is also related to future goals, hopes, and wishes, and this is reflected in the Star card.

In a love and relationship reading, the Star card indicates that past relationship issues must not be allowed to cloud the positive potential of the relationship in question or of a future relationship. Each relationship is different, so don't allow your past fears and hurts to affect future relationships.

If the query is about career and wealth, the Star card suggests new opportunities, increased abundance, and a positive outlook. A new job opportunity, promotion, raise, or surprise increase in wealth is in the cards.

For a reading related to goals and values, the Star card is an indicator of optimism about the querent's values and goals and the likelihood that they will come to fruition. It can also suggest that now is a good time to focus on goals.

If the Star comes up as a wild card, it's cause for celebration, optimism, and positivity unless the card is reversed. Renewal and peace are in the cards.

XVIII: THE MOON

THE MOON

Planet/sign: Pisces

Element: Water

Numerology: $18/9$: accomplishment

Colors: Blue, white, and gold

Symbols: Full moon, dog, wolf, water, pillars, crustacean, water, and sky/stars

Upright keywords: Intuition, subconscious, dreams, illusion, delusion, and fear

Reversed keywords: Inner confusion, releasing fears, anxiety, and lack of faith

Both the Moon and Pisces are receptive night energies and are connected to intuition, feelings, nebulous fears, and strong intuition and dreams. The recurring symbol of the pillars (related to the wisdom of Solomon) appears again in this card. The emerging consciousness of the crustacean from the water creates connection to the watery reams of Pisces and trusting the messages from the subconscious for spiritual growth. The dog and wolf represent the duality of Pisces. The symbol of two fish swimming in opposite directions represent the tamed and wild aspects of our nature, combining mind and spirit.

If the Moon card appears in a love and relationship reading, there's a call to trust inner knowing and intuition. This can also mean there is a fear of loss, insecurity, distrust, and confusion around love and relationships.

In a career and wealth reading, the Moon represents uncertainty and lack of direction. Guidance around sitting with the uncertainty and allowing the path forward to emerge is helpful when this card appears.

If the Moon appears in readings about values and goals, there's a lot of confusion and a need to go within to listen to feelings and emotional desires so that goals can come forth. It's also okay to advise moving forward even though the path is uncertain, knowing that the confusion will eventually clear.

If the Moon is a wild card, it's always a call to focus on the intuitive and the subconscious while making the querent aware that they are likely to be impressionable at this time and very empathic—easily influenced by energies surrounding them.

XIX: THE SUN

THE SUN

Planet/sign: The Sun

Element: Fire

Numerology: $19/1$: new beginnings

Colors: Blue, white, and gold

Symbols: Sun and a naked child on white horse

Upright keywords: Vitality, joy, creativity, happiness, and success

Reversed keywords: Lack of confidence, burnout, and feeling low

The Sun is the only card associated with the luminary, or planet of the same name, which makes this card fairly easy to understand. The Sun is our core, the center of our solar system, and rules Leo and the heart. The Sun itself brings light and warmth into our lives, and there's a sense of joy and increased life force when we spend some time under the Sun. This is representative of vitality, optimism, joy and general well-being, success, and happiness. The Sun and Leo are also often associated with our inner child and a sense of creativity and new beginnings.

In love and romance, the Sun card is auspicious and indicates happiness and joy. This card can also mean bringing love as a verb into your relationships, which entails being loving and radiating joy.

If the Sun card appears in a reading about career and wealth, it can indicate that new and more joyful beginnings are coming in those areas. Success is likely, and feelings of abundance and fulfilment are in the cards.

If the reading is about goals and values, the Sun card indicates that thought is required around what brings the querent feelings of happiness and joy. This is about following your bliss.

It's always lovely to pull the Sun as a wild card because it indicates a general feeling of fulfilment and happiness.

XX: JUDGMENT

JUDGMENT

Planet/sign: Pluto

Element: Fire

Numerology: $20/2$: balance

Colors: Black, white, gray, blue, and gold

Symbols: Winged angel blowing a trumpet and figures in coffins looking to angel

Upright keywords: Rebirth, review, transition, resurrection, and rite of passage

Reversed keywords: Refusal to learn from mistakes, feeling judged, and inability to let go of the past

As we near the end of the Major Arcana, we reach a card that represents a review of life's journey—a judgment of sorts—and a cycle of death and rebirth or transformation, as represented by Pluto. This planet's role in astrology is that of the excavator of both the shadow and the hidden gold within a person. Pluto reveals what is no longer needed and finds the hidden strengths within a person. This is the energy of the Judgment card. It calls for a review of life at a point of transition or death and rebirth, and the call to leave what no longer serves behind.

If Judgment appears in a love and relationship reading, a relationship is going through a period of review around what's working and what needs to change. This card can also indicate what needs to change in the querent to find a healthy relationship by looking at past relationships.

In career and wealth matters, the Judgment card generally suggests a life review before moving into a new phase or role. A look at past mistakes, where the querent can improve, and a letting go of that which didn't work as well are all advisable.

If the reading is about goals and values, the review energy is also apt, as our core values can shift over time, so goals also shift. This card encourages a thorough examination of where the querent is now and where they wish to go.

If Judgment appears as a wild card, pausing to do a life phase review is advisable. The querent is likely about to move into a new phase, so a review is necessary before moving forward.

XXI: THE WORLD

THE WORLD

Planet/sign: Saturn

Element: Earth

Numerology: $21/3$: creation

Colors: Blue, black, white, and brown

Symbols: Naked figure carrying wands/staffs suspended in the sky surrounded by a wreath and four figures in each corner, representing the four elements

Upright keywords: Completion, success, achievement, fulfilment, and accomplishment

Reversed keywords: Overwhelm, unfinished business, and inability to see accomplishment

As Saturn's cycles represent graduation from one cycle of life to another, so the World represents competition and accomplishment of one cycle of life and the beginning of another. Saturn also represents mastery, achievement, a job well done, as does the World. Congratulations are usually in order when this card is pulled. It brings a sense of maturity and completion, wholeness, and assimilation of mind, body, spirit, and action. This card represents the culmination of the Fool's journey after learning the lessons presented in life thus far while remaining mindful that the journey begins again, as there are always more lessons to master and challenges to face.

If the World appears in a love and relationship reading, it's likely that a relationship has weathered challenges and has reached a level of maturity over time. If the person is looking for love, they are likely ready for a healthy relationship.

In a career and wealth reading, the World card suggests that the querent has reached a peak of success in either area and that it's time to enjoy that success before moving on to the next phase.

In a goals and values reading, the World suggests that it's time to enjoy the fruits of the querent's labor, and then to create new goals based on the lessons learned thus far.

If the World appears as a wild card, it's an indication that it's time to pause and acknowledge completion and success in some area of life. It's time to celebrate mastery of something and the querent's accomplishments.

7

THE MINOR ARCANA: CUPS

The Major Arcana deals with bigger archetypal issues; we now turn to the Minor Arcana, which deals with more day-to-day situations. We begin by looking at the suit of cups. This suit corresponds to the element of water and the signs Cancer, Scorpio, and Pisces. It's also related to watery themes such as love, emotions, creativity, compassion, intuition, and vulnerability.

THE ACE OF CUPS

ACE OF CUPS

The ace of cups corresponds to the element of water and the three water signs, Cancer, Scorpio, and Pisces, which are ruled by the Moon, Pluto, and Neptune. Understanding these signs and rulers can help us understand that this is the energy of emotions, creativity, compassion, and relationships. The water element always indicates the emotional realm and connections. The overflowing cup, the open water lilies, and the white bird flying into the cup all suggest that this card is the spiritual and compassionate connection to love and source.

In a love and relationship reading, this card usually indicates a new love relationship or a renewed sense of love and deepening intimacy in a current one. This is a wonderful omen in this context.

If the reading is about career and wealth, the ace of cups suggests either a new emotionally fulfilling job or emotional enjoyment and fulfilment in the workplace. It can also indicate a new creative endeavor or project, and a flood of creative inspiration or creative ways to increase wealth and abundance.

If this card appears in a reading about values and goals, it indicates that emotional, compassionate, and creative goals are the focus in life right now. Clarity around relationship values and goals is in order.

Planet/sign: Cancer, Scorpio, and Pisces

Decan: Aces are not associated with a decan

Corresponding dates: Aces are not given dates

Element: Water

Numerology: 1: new beginnings

Colors: Blue, white, and gold

Symbols: Gold cup, water, water lilies, bird/dove, and cloud/hand holding a cup

Upright keywords: New beginnings, abundance of love, compassion, creativity, and new relationships

Reversed keywords: Sadness, repressed emotions, and depression

2 OF CUPS

2 OF CUPS

The signs of Cancer and Venus correspond to the two of cups, suggesting that this card is all about emotional receptivity, connection, feelings, family, and emotional balance in relationships. Venus rules love, relationships, and harmony, whereas Cancer rules the giving and receiving of love and the sense of security when emotional needs are in balance. The card shows a male and female figure facing each other and each holding one of the two cups; between them are intertwined snakes, joining the colors of the figures' clothing, which is Hermes' caduceus, bridging the world of source and humans. This leads up to a chimera figure, which combines male and feminine energies.

If the two of cups appears in a love and relationship reading, a new relationship may have a high level of emotional commitment, connection, and balance. It can also mean that a current relationship is deepening in these areas.

If the reading is about career and wealth, this card indicates mutual respect, harmony, and balance. Cancer is also connected to feeling emotionally secure, so this card bodes well for career and finances.

In a values and goals reading, the two of cups indicates that the querent's innermost emotional core values around finance, family, and career are the focus. Goals related to emotional connection and balance are likely the current focus.

Planet/sign: Cancer

Decan: Venus

Corresponding dates: Roughly June 21–July 1

Element: Water

Numerology: 2: balance

Colors: Gray, black, white, red, and gold

Symbols: Intertwined serpents (red and black and Hermes' caduceus), lion head with wings (chimera), and male and female figures holding a cup each

Upright keywords: Unity, relationships, balance, connection, and partnership

Reversed keywords: Breakups, lack of connection, lack of balance, and disagreement

3 OF CUPS

3 OF CUPS

Planet/sign: Cancer

Decan: Mercury

Corresponding dates: Roughly July 2–July 11

Element: Water

Numerology: 3: creation

Colors: Green, red, black, and yellow

Symbols: Three female dancing figures barefoot in a circle, flowers, and trees

Upright keywords: Gatherings, friendship, family bonds, celebration, and fun

Reversed keywords: Lack of friendships, canceled plans, gossip

The three of cups corresponds to the Mercury decan of Cancer, and therefore, indicates the communication and connection element contained within emotional bonds. Mercury corresponds to community, among other things, and Cancer corresponds to emotional security and connection. The three of cups represents the connections of friendship and family beyond the central partnership. This is a card of celebration and creation, as the flowers underfoot the three figures suggest freshness and fun, and the dancing indicates a celebratory event.

If the three of cups appears in a love and relationship reading, finding love through social celebrations or a friendship leading to a love relationship is possible. As Cancer is also related to family, this card could point to celebrating a birth in the family.

In a career and wealth reading, the three of cups suggests a positive, friendly, and fun community in the workplace, with supportive relationships. This card can also indicate financial or career news that is worth celebrating.

If the reading is about values and goals, there's a focus around friendships and community. Shared values and goals are represented here.

4 OF CUPS

4 OF CUPS

The four of cups corresponds to the sign of Cancer and the Moon, Cancer's ruler. Cancer is a very protective energy and needs safety and security. The figure in the card is on the ground, sitting against a tree—both symbols of secure foundations. The crossed arms are like the crab's pincers or claws, drawn together in a protective stance. Cancer's protective need for security can make them fearful of new opportunities and change. This energy is reflected in the symbolism of the card, as the figure is closed off to the outstretched hand offering a way forward. The three ignored cups on the ground also suggest apathy, boredom, and stagnation.

If the four of cups appears in a love and relationship reading, the querent may be in an emotional rut where nothing inspires passion or excitement. This could be that the querent has experienced a breakup, or that a relationship has dulled. Ignoring of the outstretched cup suggests an unwillingness to explore ways to reignite passions.

In a career or wealth reading, the four of cups suggests boredom and lack of interest in any opportunities being offered. In this context, the card points to an unwillingness to take risks and step outside of comfort zones, and a lack of gratitude by not looking at accomplishments.

If the four of cups appears in a values and goals reading, some real emotional exploration is in order to discover why the querent feels so stagnant and disillusioned. Figuring out what their core values are may help find a way forward.

Planet/sign: Cancer

Decan: Moon

Corresponding dates: Roughly July 12–July 21

Element: Water

Numerology: 4: foundation

Colors: Green, blue, and white

Symbols: Seated figure with crossed arms, a tree, an outstretched arm holding cup, and three cups on the ground

Upright keywords: Closed to opportunities, refusing offer, melancholy, unmotivated, and stuck

Reversed keywords: Motivated, open to opportunities, and reenergized

5 OF CUPS

5 OF CUPS

Planet/sign: Scorpio

Decan: Mars

Corresponding dates: Roughly Oct. 22–Oct. 31

Element: Water

Numerology: 5: change

Colors: Blue, black, and gold

Symbols: Figure with black cloak and head bowed, water, a bridge, and buildings beyond

Upright keywords: Disappointment, sadness, dejection, grief, and loneliness

Reversed keywords: Letting go, acceptance, seeing positives, and moving on

Scorpio and the sign's traditional ruler, Mars, correspond to the five of cups card. Scorpio is a water sign that is related to deep emotions and intensity, and Mars tends to cut into those emotions like a knife. The figure is cloaked in black—a color associated with Scorpio—and an indicator of a black mood. Turned away from the person looking at the card, the figure is lonely, but apparently shutting others out. Two of the cups are upright but three are tipped over, suggesting that something has been lost or "spilled." A bridge in the distance, across the water of emotions, appears to lead to a town, where other people live. However, the figure is not looking in that direction.

If the five of cups appears in a love and relationship reading, it indicates a time of emotional loss and grieving, either after a breakup or a time of tensions in a relationship. The two cups still upright and the bridge in the distance suggest looking at what good remains; there is hope that the querent can pick up the pieces and move forward.

In a career or wealth reading, the five of cups could indicate a loss of position or job, or financial losses. It suggests dejection and sadness, along with an inability to see a way forward. However, there is a way forward, whether that be regaining what was lost or a learning opportunity creating a brighter future.

The five of cups in a values and goals reading suggests that some lessons must be reflected upon so that feelings of disappointment and grief can be turned into a way to move forward.

6 OF CUPS

6 OF CUPS

The six of cups is associated with the fixed sign of Scorpio and the Sun decan, which suggests that this card has sunnier emotions than the previous one. The Sun is the core self and represents joy, the inner child, and love. In Scorpio, the Sun has deep emotions that can be somewhat "stuck," as Scorpio is a fixed sign that is often broody and likes things to stay the same. Although this card has a childlike, harmonious feel, the dark background and the five cups still on the ground can suggest the tendency to be nostalgic about the past. It can also represent the passing on of tradition from person to person or a longing to return to more harmonious times.

In a love and relationship reading, the six of cups indicates an exploration of memories in a current or past relationship or a reconnection with an old partner. This can be a fruitful time if this exploration is used to create harmony in the present and future in relationships.

If the six of cups appears in a career and wealth reading, it represents taking a look back at the path that brought the querent to where they are now so that the lessons learned can help build the future.

If the reading is about values and goals, the focus is on core values that relate to joy, traditions, and what from the past that has brought deep meaning and lit up the inner child. If the six of cups appears in this reading, some deep emotional reflection is called for.

Planet/sign: Scorpio

Decan: Sun

Corresponding dates: Roughly Nov. 1–Nov. 11

Element: Water

Numerology: 6: harmony

Colors: Green, gold, red, and black

Symbols: Flowers in the cups, male and female children, and giving a gift

Upright keywords: Childhood, inner child, joy, love, memories, nostalgia, and traditions

Reversed keywords: Stuck in the past, lack of joy, independence, and maturity

7 OF CUPS

7 OF CUPS

Planet/sign: Scorpio

Decan: Venus

Corresponding dates: Roughly Nov. 12–Nov. 21

Element: Water

Numerology: 7: reflection

Colors: Gray and white

Symbols: Clouds, floating cups, and images floating out of and around the cups

Upright keywords: Dreams, choices, illusions, fantasy, imagination, and confusion

Reversed keywords: Feeling lost, indecisiveness, lack of purpose, and chaos

Fixed sign Scorpio and the Venus decan correspond with the seven of cups card. Scorpio is the deepest of water signs and represents desire, instincts, the psyche, and emotions that are so deep they are often unacknowledged or hard to express. Venus represents the desire for love, connection, and material abundance. The card indicates hard-to-access emotions, feelings, and desires. The clouds and floating cups with different items floating around them indicate multiple dreams and desires emerging from the psyche, but also lack of clarity about those desires. This card evokes a sense of so many choices, some of which are not good because they are not grounded in reality.

If the seven of cups appears in a love and relationship reading, there's major confusion. The querent may be facing a choice between different partners or even between love and different areas of life, such as family and career. This card is a caution that nothing is clear and that the querent should not rush into anything until all options have been carefully considered.

In a career and wealth reading, the seven of cups indicates a lot of options. The career or financial path forward isn't clear. The card also suggests that the querent is stuck in indecision and confusion, not taking any practical steps in any direction. If the reading is about financial investments, some delusion and deception may be involved.

If the seven of cups appears in a goals and values reading, this card indicates a distinct lack of clarity and indecisiveness. Venus represents values, but this person is not at all clear on their values and must do some soul-searching to figure out what they really desire and if it's even practical.

8 OF CUPS

8 OF CUPS

The sign of Pisces and the Saturn decan correspond to the eight of cups card. Pisces is a mutable (change) sign that is vulnerable, idealistic, and very emotional. Meanwhile, Saturn represents boundaries, drawing a line, and mastery. As this suggests, this indicates that the eight of cups means drawing emotional boundaries and moving on from unfulfilling emotional situations. The figure is walking away from the cups, leaving them on the ground while striding purposefully uphill to a new start. The full moon in the card also indicates fulfilment and release of that which is no longer working. The Moon is also about emotions.

In a love and relationship reading, the eight of cups represents leaving emotionally unfulfilling relationships behind and having the strength to move on. The card can also indicate leaving unhealthy emotional patterns and fears behind after working through issues.

If the eight of cups appears in a career or wealth reading, it suggests that doing things the way they have always been done is draining and exhausting the querent, and it's time to do things differently. This could be just taking a break to refresh or walking away from a job. It can also mean cutting losses in an investment and working toward wiser investments.

In a goal and values reading, this card suggests a need to get clear on what is emotionally fulfilling and to leave behind anything that isn't. By getting crystal clear on values and boundaries, much more courageous goals will be created.

Planet/sign: Pisces

Decan: Saturn

Corresponding dates: Roughly Feb. 21–March 1

Element: Water

Numerology: 8: mastery

Colors: Blue, black, and gold

Symbols: Figure dressed in black walking away and uphill, a full moon, mountains, and water

Upright keywords: Walking away, letting go, courage, and leaving behind

Reversed keywords: Clinging on, stagnation, inability to let go, and fear of change/moving on

9 OF CUPS

9 OF CUPS

Planet/sign: Pisces

Decan: Jupiter

Corresponding dates: Roughly March 2–March 10

Element: Water

Numerology: 9: accomplishment

Colors: Blue, black, and brown

Symbols: Figure sitting solidly on a bench and nine cups overhead

Upright keywords: Fulfilled wishes, rewards, contentment, happiness, recognition, and success

Reversed keywords: Unhappiness, lack of fulfillment, pessimism, negativity, and unfulfilled wishes

The nine of cups corresponds to Pisces and the Jupiter decan, two energies that work very well together, as Jupiter is the traditional ruler of Pisces. This sign is about faith, compassion, and oneness, and is a dreamy sign. Jupiter is the planet of expansion, optimism, aspirations, luck, and abundance. In the card, the figure sits solidly with arms crossed in a posture of contentment. The nine cups above the figure's head indicate a peak of success, and that's what this card means. It brings forth feelings of gratitude for the attainment of success in some area and feeling lucky, positive, and accomplished.

If the nine of cups appears in a love and relationship reading, this is an indication of positivity and a fulfilling love life. This card is cause for celebration because wishes are coming true, evoking feelings of happiness and contentment.

In a career and wealth reading, the nine of cups indicates a time of personal achievement and satisfaction. It may also suggest a raise or promotion and recognition of efforts. In finances, it indicates rewards and financial abundance.

If the reading is about values and goals, the nine of cups means taking stock and expressing gratitude for all that has been achieved before racing onto the next goals. It's time to take a pause and feel content that life is good.

10 OF CUPS

10 OF CUPS

Planet/sign: Pisces

Decan: Mars

Corresponding dates: Roughly March 11–March 20

Element: Water

Numerology: 10: completion

Colors: Blue, green, gold, and red

Symbols: Family playing in celebratory fashion, home, trees, and 10 cups overhead

Upright keywords: Family, happiness, emotional fulfilment, abundance, and harmony

Reversed keywords: Unhappy home, domestic conflict, disharmony, and unhappiness

The ten of cups is the last of the numbered cards in the suit. It represents completion, a life well lived, and the attainment of success. The cups suit is the water suit and therefore represents emotional fulfilment and joy. The sign of Pisces and the Mars decan correspond to this card, suggesting forward movement (Mars). This card is about completion but not standing still; rather, it's about reaching a point of happiness and stability that is cause for celebration. Moving forward with this emotional stability is possible now. The children playing with joy, the couple with their arms raised in jubilation as they look at the fruits of the labor, and the home they have created together speak to this. The overhead cups crown their achievements.

In a love and relationship reading, the ten of cups indicates a sense of delight and wholeness in relationships. This may mean taking the next step in a relationship or introducing a love interest into your family. The ten of cups is a sign of a long-lasting relationship that will bring great happiness.

If the reading is about career and wealth, the ten of cups suggests an emotionally fulfilling career, a supportive and friendly work environment, and a general sense of financial stability and harmony. This card can also indicate the end of a career through retirement or leaving the job to focus on caring for the family and home.

If the ten of cups appears in a reading focused on values and goals, it suggests that creating a family and a loving, stable home life are what is desired. The querent should set the intention to create that by attracting a relationship with someone who shares their core values.

THE PAGE OF CUPS

PAGE OF CUPS

Planet/sign: All water and earth signs—Cancer, Scorpio, Pisces, Taurus, Virgo, and Capricorn

Decan: No decan

Corresponding dates: No dates

Element: Water/earth

Numerology: No number

Colors: Red, gold, blue, and gray

Symbols: Walking figure carrying a cup, a fish appearing from cup, red clothing, and the seashore

Upright keywords: Dreamer, sensitivity, inner child, head in the clouds, and idealism

Reversed keywords: Immaturity, broken dreams, and emotional vulnerability

The Page of cups is the energy of earth and water. It represents an emotional awakening of sorts, as the figure is walking on the shifting sands at the water's edge staring intently at the fish emerging from the cup. The blending of grounded earth with the fluidity of water speak to the formation of new projects. This suggests being open to inspiration and new ideas that come from intuition. The fish is out of water, as if to remind the figure to look to the watery energy of emotional and intuitive creation to find a new perspective and way forward.

In a love and relationship reading, the Page of cups can indicate a person coming into the querent's life with a naive, fun, and childlike demeanor. It can suggest that the querent lighten up and take a lighter and more playful approach to finding a partner. In an existing relationship, the Page of cups indicates a new sense of sensitivity and joy.

If the Page of cups appears in a career and wealth reading, it might suggest that the querent should pursue a field that uses their creative talents. It can also mean that their career and financial dreams are somewhat unrealistic and that they need a reality check to get more grounded.

In a values and goals reading, the Page of cups suggests that the querent is being asked to stretch beyond their comfort zones and current circumstances to new possibilities and dreams.

THE KNIGHT OF CUPS

KNIGHT OF CUPS

Planet/sign: All water and air signs—Cancer, Scorpio, Pisces, Gemini, Libra, and Aquarius

Decan: No decan

Corresponding dates: No dates

Element: Water/air

Numerology: No number

Colors: White, blue, and gold

Symbols: Knight, holding cup aloft, white horse, and seashore

Upright keywords: Follow your heart, charming, artistic ability, romance, and creativity

Reversed keywords: Moodiness, turmoil, disappointment, and lack of creativity

The Knight of cups corresponds to the elements of water and air. Mixed with water, wind (or air) tends to make waves, lending the Knight of cups forward movement, as seen in the emotional waves of creative ideas and charm moving forward on the white horse, a symbol of purity of intention and energy or power. The Knight of cups has emotions and ideas in strong balance. This can represent the querent or a person that brings these energies into their life, such as a messenger that invites the querent to follow their heart.

In a love and relationship reading, the Knight of cups is an indication that love is on the horizon, but this can be an over-idealized romance or one that has unrealistic expectations.

If the Knight of cups appears in a career and wealth reading, this card has more of a diplomatic edge and represents the ability to mediate with compassion in work conflicts. It can also suggest creative solutions and projects.

If the reading is about values and goals, then the Knight of cups invites the querent to focus their attention on their creative and love desires. What do they really desire if they follow their heart?

THE QUEEN OF CUPS

QUEEN OF CUPS

Planet/sign: All water signs—
Cancer, Scorpio, and Pisces

Decan: No decan

Corresponding dates: No dates

Element: Water/water

Numerology: No number

Colors: White, blue, and gold

Symbols: Female figure in
gold holding cup aloft, throne,
and water

Upright keywords: Caring,
empathy, kindheartedness,
counselor, and healer

Reversed keywords: Insecurity,
depression, lacking direction,
and neediness

The Queen of cups is associated with a pure water element, which indicates that this is the epitome of nurturing, compassionate, and healing energy. The female figure on the card is sitting crossed-legged in a very relaxed, peaceful, and contemplative position on the throne wearing a gold gown—the color of wisdom and love—and crown, and is holding the cup aloft and looking at it, suggesting loving focus and abundance. The cup is lidded, symbolizing an internal, unconscious focus. The throne appears to be on water, with the water of the astrological element and the card representing intuition and feelings. The throne has shells and fish behind the figure, further emphasizing the water element.

If the Queen of cups appears in a love and relationship reading, it suggests that there is deep love in the cards or deeper love in a current relationship. Either someone embodying these traits is coming into the querent's life, or the querent themselves is embodying these traits and attracting love. Caution around strong boundaries is necessary, as this energy can attract the overly needy.

In a career and wealth reading, the Queen of cups is a reminder that emotional fulfilment in the workplace and/or in financial gain is an important factor. In career, this could represent the querent pursuing a more emotionally fulfilling career or even a nurturing career. It can also indicate seeking out someone who provides this energy in the workplace.

If the reading is about values and goals, the Queen of cups is a clear indicator that emotionally fulfilling values should be the focus and that relationship goals center around the kind of relationships that are desired.

THE KING OF CUPS

KING OF CUPS

Planet/sign: All water and fire signs—Cancer, Scorpio, Pisces, Aries, Leo, and Sagittarius

Decan: No decan

Corresponding dates: No dates

Element: Water/fire

Numerology: No number

Colors: White and blue

Symbols: Male figure on throne, scepter, cup, and water

Upright keywords: Maturity, compassion, counselor/advisor, diplomacy, and wisdom

Reversed keywords: Lack of caring, selfishness, emotional immaturity, and anxiety

As a mix of water and fire, the King of cups brings a balance between emotion and action—the heart and head. Therefore, it represents a person that embodies both emotional and intellectual wisdom. This can mean a person in the querent's life or the querent themselves, and indicates a high level of emotional maturity and balance. The figure on the card sits in a very balanced, strong stance on the throne, holding an orbed scepter and an open cup. The golden crown and the scepter symbolize power and authority, but the figure wears a fish amulet and there are fish on the throne. This is one that is in charge of their emotions and yet is very open and loving, indicative of a strong but sensitive leader.

In a love and relationship reading, the King of cups signifies balancing the heart and head when looking for love and not allowing yourself to get swept away by emotion alone. This can also point to a relationship with an emotionally mature person.

If the King of cups appears in a career and wealth reading, the card suggests both career and financial stability. In the workplace, it could mean an emotionally mature and experienced mentor who can serve as a guide in developing those same qualities.

If the reading is about values and goals, the King of cups is a suggestion to focus both the intellect and the emotions to get clear on core values and create goals that are balanced with both heart and mind.

8

THE MINOR ARCANA: PENTACLES

We next look at the suit of pentacles (also sometimes called disks or coins). Pentacles is the earth suit, and as such, it is associated with earth signs Taurus, Virgo, and Capricorn, as well as earthly themes such as finances, material security, skills, career, achievements through hard work, the physical home, and the body.

THE ACE OF PENTACLES

ACE OF PENTACLES

Planet/sign: Taurus, Virgo, and Capricorn

Decan: Aces are not associated with a decan

Corresponding dates: Aces are not given dates

Element: Earth

Numerology: 1: new beginnings

Colors: Green, black, white, and gold

Symbols: Cloud/hand holding pentagram, flowers, and grass

Upright keywords: New beginnings, material gain, new business, reward, and new responsibility

Reversed keywords: Caution regarding financial decisions, unwise choices, and lack of grounding

An understanding of the energies of the Earth signs—Taurus, Virgo, and Capricorn—and their rulers—Venus, Mercury, and Saturn—demonstrates that the ace of pentacles is associated with the material world and our physical selves. Think of the physical senses and themes associated with earth signs—the body, work, and achievement for example—to get a sense of the pentacles. Given that the ace always points to new beginnings, that will give you a guide to start interpreting the card.

If the ace of pentacles is pulled in a love and relationship reading, it suggests a sense of material abundance and new responsibilities in those areas. It can also indicate a new, stable relationship or a new air of stability in a current relationship.

In a career and wealth reading, the ace of pentacles is a wonderful card to pull, as it indicates new beginnings and/or new responsibilities in these areas. This could mean starting a business, entering a new investment opportunity, or even getting an inheritance.

If goals and values are the focus of the reading, this card suggests guiding the querent to create goals based on strong financial and career values.

2 OF PENTACLES

2 OF PENTACLES

Planet/sign: Capricorn

Decan: Jupiter

Corresponding dates: Roughly Dec. 21–Dec. 30

Element: Earth

Numerology: 2: balance

Colors: Green, blue, gray, gold, and sand

Symbols: Earth, water, figure juggling two pentagrams, infinity/balance symbol, and boats

Upright keywords: Juggling, finding balance during change, and setting things in motion

Reversed keywords: Lack of balance, lack of planning/organization, and juggling too many things

Jupiter is the planet of expansion and belief, and Capricorn corresponds to boundaries, determination, and diligence. This indicates what the two of pentacles means. As the journey through the pentacles began with the ace, the two is about finding balance between expansion and strong boundaries, or not taking on too much while also moving forward with determination. Hence, the balance message of the card is about equilibrium of opposing energies.

If this card appears in a query about love and relationships, it could indicate that there's an imbalance between two people and that equilibrium needs to be worked on. It could be a message to balance love/work life or a message that the querent is juggling responsibilities.

In a career and wealth reading, the card indicates that the querent might be juggling too many projects and responsibilities, or that they are taking on extra responsibilities that require adjustments.

If the two of pentacles appears in a reading around goals and values, it's a call to think carefully about work/life balance when creating goals, making them based on solid values (Capricorn), but also stretching slightly beyond their comfort zone (Jupiter).

3 OF PENTACLES

3 OF PENTACLES

Planet/sign: Capricorn

Decan: Mars

Corresponding dates: Roughly Dec. 31–Jan. 10

Element: Earth

Numerology: 3: creation

Colors: Black, white, blue, and gold

Symbols: A carpenter-type figure sculpting an arch, and a man and woman holding plans

Upright keywords: Teamwork, collaboration, creation, and learning

Reversed keywords: Lack of commitment, lack of collaboration, and conflict in a team

Mars is the planet of action and willfulness, and Capricorn is the sign of steady achievement and slow building. The two can work well together, as Mars pushes Capricorn to move and to grow. However, Mars can also be very much the leader and like things done a certain way. In that respect, Capricorn slows Mars down and asks them to listen to others. This is how collaboration works best—the coming together of individuals (Mars) to achieve common goals (Capricorn).

In a love and relationship reading, the three of pentacles suggests pulling together to create something. It is about bringing different strengths into the relationship and listening to each other to work at your best.

If the reading is about career and wealth, the three of pentacles indicates teamwork in the workplace or a collaborative investment with everyone bringing their skills to work together.

If the three of pentacles is pulled in a goals and values reading, it suggests that the querent is being asked to collaborate with those who share common values.

4 OF PENTACLES

4 OF PENTACLES

Planet/sign: Capricorn

Decan: Sun

Corresponding dates: Roughly Jan. 11–Jan. 20

Element: Earth

Numerology: 4: foundation

Colors: Black, white, gray, purple, and gold

Symbols: Figure sitting balanced on seat, balancing the four pentagrams perfectly with two underfoot and buildings in background

Upright keywords: Security, saving, planning, holding onto things, or someone holding onto the querent

Reversed keywords: Sharing, giving, lack of financial security, and lack of planning

Moving onto the numbers that correspond to the fixed signs, we begin with the four of pentacles, which corresponds to the Sun and Taurus. The Sun is our core self, and Taurus is associated with the material world, with money, resources, the physical home, and possessions. The four of pentacles, therefore, is all about security and foundations in the material world, and about the preservation of resources. The figure balancing the four pentagrams appears to be holding on tightly, so that there's not only stability, but also so no one can take them away.

In a love and relationship reading, the querent is likely looking for a stable relationship, perhaps with someone with Capricorn energy, or to build financial stability in an existing relationship.

If the reading is about career and wealth, this is a good omen for stability in the career or for investments, with a slight caution that there might be a fear of taking any risks and holding on too tightly to what the querent currently has.

If this is a goals and values reading, the querent should be asked to get very clear on what goals will make them feel secure to focus on creating stability and security in their lives. This also suggests that this is a core value for them at this time.

5 OF PENTACLES

5 OF PENTACLES

The five of pentacles corresponds to Mercury, the planet of change, messages, communication, and trickery, as well as with Taurus, the sign of material resources and comfort zones. This card suggests a change of fortune, perhaps falling on hard times or feeling a sense of futility and lack of direction, as if hard work is achieving nothing. As Mercury is the planet of the mind, this often indicates mental stress, a lot of worry, and a strong inner critical voice telling the querent that they haven't done enough or blaming themselves for the hard times. The light in the window on the card goes unnoticed by the figures as if to say that they can't see the light or way forward right now.

In a love and relationship reading, the five of pentacles could indicate some strife and arguments over financial hard times or lack of direction—perhaps one partner is laying more blame on the other. A meeting of the minds is called for here to move forward.

If the card comes up in a reading about career and wealth, it always means financial difficulties or feelings of futility around lack of progress after hard work. It could also point to a lack of direction. The querent may not be giving themselves any credit for what they have achieved; a suggestion to think about what they are grateful for right now will help.

If the reading is about goals and values, the five of pentacles suggests a lack of direction and clarity around core values. The querent may need guidance in thinking about what their values are to create goals from that.

Planet/sign: Taurus

Decan: Mercury

Corresponding dates: Roughly April 21–April 30

Element: Earth

Numerology: 5: change

Colors: Gray, blue, and gold

Symbols: Two figures, snow, and an unnoticed window lit with five pentagrams

Upright keywords: Hardship, isolation, lack, lack of gratitude for what you have, and depression

Reversed keywords: Progress, positive change, and overcoming hardship

6 OF PENTACLES

6 OF PENTACLES

Planet/sign: Taurus

Decan: Moon

Corresponding dates: Roughly May 1–May 10

Element: Earth

Numerology: 6: harmony

Colors: Green, gold, black, white, and gray

Symbols: Figure with crown juggling pentagrams, scales, and a kneeling figure with hands held out

Upright keywords: Sharing to create balance, kindness, equality, reciprocity, and receiving

Reversed keywords: Inequality, lack of reciprocity, hoarding resources, and unwilling to accept support

The Moon in Taurus corresponds to the six of pentacles. The Moon speaks to our emotions, moods, and inner security. Taurus is the sign of material self-worth, security, physical affection, and comfort. This card exudes material well-being and harmony, but the Moon itself is a receptive, reciprocal energy, having no light of its own. In other words, the Moon shines brightest when it receives the light of the Sun. This card is all about sharing the wealth, of being prepared to both give and receive abundance, and to live in a reciprocal relationship with others and the Earth.

If the six of pentacles appears in a love and relationship reading, this card suggests emotional connection and sharing of all abundance between partners. This applies to all forms of abundance, including emotional generosity and receiving support and love.

In a reading around career and wealth, the six of pentacles indicates a feeling of sharing and generosity of all forms of wealth and abundance. It calls for being willing to both give and receive all resources and to create a mutual sense of abundance.

If the six of pentacles appears in a goals and values reading, the card suggests creating an inventory of gratitude for what the person has so they can share that abundance with others and create goals based on sharing of abundance moving forward.

7 OF PENTACLES

7 OF PENTACLES

Planet/sign: Taurus

Decan: Saturn

Corresponding dates: Roughly May 11–May 20

Element: Earth

Numerology: 7: reflection

Colors: Green, gold, and brown

Symbols: Contemplative figure holding harvesting tool, six pentagrams on bush, and one pentagram at the figure's feet

Upright keywords: Rewards, patience, cultivation, waiting to harvest, and perseverance

Reversed keywords: Giving up, impatience, repeating mistakes, and not seeing rewards

The seven of pentacles corresponds to the Saturn decan of Taurus and represents rewards for hard work that are almost ready to harvest. This is the last of the fixed sign cards (five through seven) before cards that bring movement forward. Saturn is related to mastery and achievement, a sense of having climbed a mountain, being diligent, and working very hard. Taurus is about the material abundance or rewards after that hard work. In this card, the figure is waiting, standing solidly on the ground as Saturn in fixed Taurus suggests. Rewards are in sight and are beginning to arrive, but patience is called for before harvesting all the rewards.

If the seven of pentacles is pulled in a love and relationship reading, it suggests that some work and patience are required in a relationship or that love might be slow to grow but that it will be lasting when it does. This can suggest a friendship growing into love, perhaps with an older person.

In a career and wealth reading, the card indicates using patience to reap the rewards of all the hard work that has been put in. Progress is being made and the rewards are in sight; the querent is on the right path.

If the seven of pentacles appears in a values and goals reading, this is a call to get very clear on values around wealth, self-worth, and abundance (Taurus), and to create solid long-term goals that work over a length of time. This is not instant manifestation energy.

8 OF PENTACLES

8 OF PENTACLES

Planet/sign: Virgo

Decan: Sun

Corresponding dates: Roughly Aug. 22–Aug. 31

Element: Mutable modality

Numerology: 8: mastery

Colors: Gray, black, brown, purple, and gold

Symbols: Figure with crafting tool crafting a pentagram, seven pentagrams floating, and houses

Upright keywords: Skills, talents, craftsmanship, precision, commitment, and dedication

Reversed keywords: Carelessness, lack of attention to detail, low quality, and low work ethic

The eight of pentacles corresponds to the first of the mutable numbered cards and the mutable earth sign, Virgo. The eight corresponds to the Sun decan of Virgo. The Sun is our innate character, our vitality, and essence. Virgo is the sign associated with service, discrimination, humility, wholeness, and self-improvement. In the card, the figure is crafting detail on one of the eight pentagrams and is very intent on the details of the card, while the other seven pentagrams float around the figure, seemingly complete and surrounding the figure to suggest wholeness.

In a love and relationship reading, the eight of pentacles means efforts to cultivate a strong relationship. Long-term relationships require humility and a willingness to improve the self and to attend to details when issues arise. This card suggests that the querent is on track in that respect and has learned to love and respect all that the partner is.

If the card appears in a career and wealth reading, it indicates dedication to improving skills and to growing expertise. This can mean a new course of study of some kind and always indicates attention to detail and maybe a promotion.

In a goals and values reading, it calls for a focus on a period of self-improvement and on goals. It suggests a time of prudence.

9 OF PENTACLES

9 OF PENTACLES

Planet/sign: Virgo

Decan: Venus

Corresponding dates: Roughly Sept. 1–Sept. 10

Element: Earth

Numerology: 9: accomplishment

Colors: Gold, purple, green, black, and white

Symbols: Figure in gold, bird on arm, pentagrams, and grapes/ vines around figure

Upright keywords: Abundance, prosperity, independence, confidence, and wisdom

Reversed keywords: Unstable finances, lack of security, and overindulgence

The nine of pentacles corresponds to the sign of Virgo and the Venus decan. Virgo is the sign associated with service, daily work, and practical usefulness. Venus corresponds with abundance, manifestation, the law of attraction, and values. In this card, the figure is surrounded by the fruits of their labor and has a regal stance and demeanor. The presence of the raptor bird on the arm is a sign of royalty. It also suggests reaching a level of wisdom in their work and mastery of a skill (falconry is a skillful pursuit). The grapes are a symbol of abundant harvest, and the sign of Virgo also corresponds to harvest.

If the nine of pentacles appears in a love and relationship reading, personal wholeness and well-being that isn't dependent on a partner or love interest is indicated. If already in a relationship, this card suggests personal fulfilment and a sense of working side by side to create prosperity.

In a career and wealth reading, the card tells us that hard work is paying off and that a level of achievement has been reached. It can also suggest pausing to take an inventory of the level of success reached and taking time to enjoy the abundance gained.

In a goals and values reading, this is a call to examine (Virgo) values around work ethic and what abundance means for the querent. It's also about setting goals according to that. What does success mean in terms of a life with meaning?

10 OF PENTACLES

10 OF PENTACLES

Planet/sign: Virgo

Decan: Mercury

Corresponding dates: Roughly Sept. 11–Sept. 21

Element: Earth

Numerology: 10: completion

Colors: Green, gold, black, and white

Symbols: Family, elder, arch, trees, and pets

Upright keywords: Fulfilment, inheritance, family foundations, family success, and abundance

Reversed keywords: Disagreement in the family over wealth and inheritances, and broken promises

The ten of pentacles is the last of the numbered cards in the pentacles suit and corresponds with completion. As a Virgo card in the Mercury decan with Mercury ruling Virgo, this card calls for an inventory of life's achievements and accomplishments. Mercury also corresponds to contracts of some kind, which can suggest a will or inheritance. The phrase "making a list and checking it twice" comes to mind, as a gratitude inventory is made for what's been accomplished in all areas of life.

If the ten of pentacles appears in a love and relationship reading, it indicates a strong bond that brings affection, a solid sense of family, and emotional fulfilment. If single, the querent is likely looking for someone with whom to create a strong family bond and who will fit into their extended family.

In career and wealth matters, the card corresponds with material success, abundance, and the creation of something lasting. This can mean a family business or a solid position in a long-standing traditional setting.

In a values and goals reading, the card corresponds with a focus on what the querent's values are around abundance in a family and relationship sense.

THE PAGE OF PENTACLES

PAGE OF PENTACLES

Planet/sign: All earth signs—Taurus, Virgo, and Capricorn

Decan: No decan

Corresponding dates: No dates

Element: Earth/earth

Numerology: No number

Colors: Purple, green, brown, and gray

Symbols: Young figure focused on and carrying a pentagram and walking, mountains, flowers underfoot, and trees

Upright keywords: New financial opportunities, grounded, growth, and a good news bearer

Reversed keywords: Bad news, the bearer of bad news, and lack of passion

The court cards correspond to the elements rather than any one sign, planetary body, decan, or a date range, and usually represent a person or the querent themselves. The Page of pentacles corresponds to the Earth and earth element, according to the Order of the Golden Dawn. Therefore, it has a major focus on material, earthly, and physical matters, hence the focus of the figure on the pentagram as the figure walks among the natural world. This speaks to a budding interest in the creation of abundance and the initial blossoming of ideas.

In a love and relationship reading, the Page of pentacles can suggest a new love that has a quiet and grounded but loyal demeanor. It has a very earthy energy that might not set the world alight but will be hardworking and focused. For those already in a relationship, the Page of pentacles represents a very loyal and supportive partner.

If the Page of pentacles appears in a career and wealth reading, it can mean a new career path or a course of higher study that will lead to career advancement. It can also mean that someone in the querent's life is offering a new opportunity.

In a values and goals reading, the Page of pentacles corresponds to clarity around values in relation to career, material abundance, and material growth. It also suggests setting goals to create new opportunities or to be open to new opportunities that are presented to you.

THE KNIGHT OF PENTACLES

The Knight of pentacles corresponds to the elements of air and earth, which indicates movement (air) around practical, material elements. The Knight is moving forward on the horse, a symbol of strength, motion, and vitality. Air pushes the figure forward following the new opportunities provided by the Page. The pentagram is held forward at arm's length and up, as if to allow the air to push it forward. The Knight and horse travel on barren ground, as if to suggest that diligence and work are called for so that progress can be made.

If the Knight of pentacles is drawn in a love and relationship reading, it can indicate the type of partner that is either in the relationship or that the querent is looking for—a steady, reliable, and supportive partner that works with the querent toward a stable future together.

In a career and wealth reading, the Knight of pentacles corresponds to slow, steady commitment to advancement in either area. This is a card that speaks of dedication, hard work, and focus.

If the Knight of pentacles appears in a reading about values and goals, the card suggests that solid and progressive values and goals are in the cards. Goals should be practical and long-term, requiring patience.

Planet/sign: Earth and air signs—Taurus, Virgo, Capricorn, Gemini, Libra, and Aquarius

Decan: No decan

Corresponding dates: No dates

Element: Earth/air

Numerology: No number

Colors: Gray, black, brown, and green

Symbols: Armored figure riding a gray horse, a pentagram held up and forward, and trees

Upright keywords: Steady progress, diligence, staying the course, patience, and practicality

Reversed keywords: Workaholic, gambling, risk-taking, and lack of initiative

THE QUEEN OF PENTACLES

QUEEN OF PENTACLES

Planet/sign: Water and earth signs—Cancer, Scorpio, Pisces, Taurus, Virgo, and Capricorn

Decan: No decan

Corresponding dates: No dates

Element: Earth/water

Numerology: No number

Colors: Purple, green, gold, black, and white

Symbols: Crowned regal female figure, grapes, flowers, throne, and rabbit

Upright keywords: Mother archetype, nurturing, warmth, groundedness, financial stability, and security

Reversed keywords: Instability, impracticality, shallowness, and ungroundedness

The yin elements of water and earth correspond to the Queen of pentacles, and water and earth together often make things that can be sculpted into practical uses. This is the energy of earthly creation and nurturing that comes from material things. The Queen sits on a white (purity of intention) and green (nature) throne, looking intently and lovingly at the pentagram in her hand, surrounded by abundance. A white rabbit, a symbol of birth, is at her side. This is the embodiment of nurturing love, and either represents a person in the querent's life or the querent themselves.

In a love and relationship reading, the Queen of pentacles corresponds to a generous, loving, kind, and nurturing relationship or person. This could indicate a couple setting up a nurturing and stable home together, an abundant period, or a very loving time in a relationship. If looking for love, the card represents the qualities for which the querent is searching.

If the Queen of pentacles is pulled in a career and wealth reading, it is a wonderful omen and indicates great success, a feeling of strong self-worth, or a loving mentor-type figure that will help in matters related to career and wealth.

In a values and goals reading, the Queen of pentacles may indicate that a lot of self-nurturing and self-love is called for. It suggests that home, abundance, and caring should be a priority at this time.

THE KING OF PENTACLES

KING OF PENTACLES

Planet/sign: Earth and fire signs—Taurus, Virgo, Capricorn, Aries, Leo, and Sagittarius

Decan: No decan

Corresponding dates: No dates

Element: Earth/fire

Numerology: No number

Colors: Purple, green, gold, black, and white

Symbols: Crowned male figure, scepter, throne, and grapes

Upright keywords: Material success, wealth, prosperity, fulfilment, and leadership

Reversed keywords: Instability, unsupportiveness, poor leadership, and materialism

The last, but not least, of the suit of pentacles is the King, a mix of fire and earth, bringing strength, resiliency, leadership, and creativity into the mix. Both fire and earth signs tend to have more natural leadership qualities, and all can be patriarchal in nature, having a fatherly tone. In the Tarot, the King is dressed in regal purple and sits on the throne, looking directly at the person looking at the card. Holding the scepter in one hand is indicative of material authority, whereas the pentagram in the other indicates spiritual authority. This is the embodiment of leadership and success, whether it indicates the querent or a person in the querent's life.

If the King of pentacles appears in a love and relationship reading, it indicates a serious, secure, and stable relationship or a relationship with a person who embodies these qualities and who will be a strong and supportive partner.

In a career and wealth reading, the King of pentacles indicates success and achievement in a career or business venture. The card can also suggest a powerful mentor who will help the querent achieve success in a career or business venture.

If the reading is about values and goals, it's time to aim for leadership and success, and to be firm about values such as stability and confidence. Firmness also helps regarding what prosperity means for the querent.

9

THE MINOR ARCANA: SWORDS

We now turn to the Minor Arcana suit of swords. This suit corresponds to the element of air; the signs Gemini, Libra, and Aquarius; and air themes such as intellect, thought, communication, logic, communication, and rationality. Air also corresponds to inventiveness and sociability but can also be aloof, scattered, and superficial at times.

THE ACE OF SWORDS

ACE OF SWORDS

Planet/sign: Gemini, Libra, and Aquarius

Decan: Aces are not associated with a decan

Corresponding dates: Aces are not given dates

Element: Air

Numerology: 1: new beginnings

Colors: Gray, black, white, and green

Symbols: Cloud/hand holding a balanced and double-edged sword, a gold crown, dangling wreath, and mountains

Upright keywords: New beginnings, new ideas, breakthrough, clear communication, and truth

Reversed keywords: Miscommunication, arguments, confusion, and injustice

The ace of swords corresponds to the element of air and its signs, Gemini, Libra, and Aquarius, which are ruled by Mercury, Venus, Uranus (modern), and Saturn (modern). This brings the energy of thought, communication, ideas, inventiveness, and mental connection, as the air element always indicates the intellectual and objective realm. The double-edged, balanced sword pointing upward from the cloud/hand, the gold crown, and the dangling wreath all suggest that this card corresponds to the mind that is overflowing with ideas that come from a connection to source. Also represented with all air element signs is a duality of opposing ideas, choices, and decisions to be made.

In a love and relationship reading, the ace of swords usually indicates a relationship where there is a meeting of minds and clear communication. It can also mean heated discussion and decisions waiting to be made. As this is a sword, the card can also mean cutting people out who are toxic.

If the reading is about career and wealth, the ace of swords suggests either a new intellectually challenging and fulfilling job or promotion. It can also indicate clarity around career goals and financial decisions and choices.

If the ace of swords appears in a reading that is connected to values and goals, it likely indicates that intellectual, social, and perhaps study goals require examination.

2 OF SWORDS

2 OF SWORDS

Planet/sign: Libra

Decan: Moon

Corresponding dates: Roughly Sept. 21–Sept. 30

Element: Air

Numerology: 2: balance

Colors: Gray, white, black, and blue

Symbols: Seated and blindfolded figure holding crossed swords, gray land, water, mountains, and moon behind

Upright keywords: Crossroads, difficult choices, inability to see a path, and blocked emotions

Reversed keywords: Anxiety, indecision, stress, and turmoil

The sign of Libra and the Moon correspond to the two of swords, and this suggests that this is all about difficult intellectual choices that are affecting the querent emotionally (the Moon). Libra rules balance, justice, and harmony, whereas the Moon rules emotional responses. This suggests that this card combines the desire for balance with those emotional responses. The card shows a lone female figure dressed in white (innocence) and blindfolded, holding two swords crossed in different directions, illustrating the inability to make a choice or to think clearly. The water and Moon behind her reflect the lack of emotional clarity or blocked emotions.

If the two of swords appears in a love and relationship reading, it indicates that perhaps a choice between two partners must be made or that there is a stalemate and indecision around a current relationship. It can also indicate a crossing of swords between two people, with each unable to hear the other clearly.

If the reading is a career and wealth reading, the two of swords suggests conflicts in the work environment and a possibility that the querent is being asked to take sides but feels anxious about doing so. Financially, this card suggests an unwillingness to look clearly at financial matters.

In a values and goals reading, the two of swords indicates that intellectual and social values and goals are the focus. In this context, this card points to a lack of clarity around which direction is best to pursue those goals.

3 OF SWORDS

3 OF SWORDS

Planet/sign: Libra

Decan: Saturn

Corresponding dates: Roughly Oct. 1–Oct. 10

Element: Air

Numerology: 3: creation

Colors: Red, white, blue, black, and gray

Symbols: Red heart floating in the air pierced by three swords

Upright keywords: Heartbreak, separation, misunderstandings, grief, and rejection

Reversed keywords: Forgiveness, compromise, reconciliation, and conflict resolution

The three of swords corresponds to the Saturn decan of Libra, and therefore, indicates blocks and sadness in communication and relationships. Saturn corresponds to limitations and restriction, and Libra corresponds to all relationships, interpersonal and intellectual. Through this, we can see that the three of swords represents restriction and blocks within relationships, as illustrated by the heart being pierced by the swords, as well as the ungrounded, floating heart. It's as if the heart feels both pierced and cast adrift.

If the three of swords appears in a love and relationship reading, it likely points to a time of strife and endings in relationships. It can indicate breakups, a third party, or past relationship patterns causing blocks to communications or barriers to relationship harmony. Like most swords cards, the message is more positive when reversed.

In a career and wealth reading, the three of swords suggests conflict of some kind in the workplace. This card can point to redundancies, firings, or business failures. Saturn always represents hard lessons or reality checks, and ultimately, this can be turned around if the lessons are heeded.

If the reading is about values and goals when the three of swords appears, there's a focus on conflict resolution, management, and personal boundaries in all significant relationships.

4 OF SWORDS

4 OF SWORDS

Planet/sign: Libra

Decan: Jupiter

Corresponding dates: Roughly Oct. 11–Oct. 20

Element: Air

Numerology: 4: foundation

Colors: Black, white, and blue

Symbols: Figured resting on a tomb engraved with a sword, three swords hung on wall, and a peaceful scene through window

Upright keywords: Deep rest, solitude, mental restoration, peace, and recuperation

Reversed keywords: Burnout, mental overload, lack of self-care, release from isolation, and restlessness

The four of swords corresponds to the sign of Libra and the Jupiter decan. Libra is related to balance, harmony, and peace, whereas Jupiter represents expansiveness and grace, especially as the traditional ruler of Pisces. The figure in the card is lying in deep rest on a tomb, which has one of the four swords depicted on the card engraved on it, while the other three swords hang on the wall. The figure has laid down their swords in deep rest to bring balance and a return to grace. This suggests a need to pause and spend some time in solitude to calm the mind and chaos of the world and recuperate.

If the four of swords appears in a love and relationship reading, it suggests taking a break from dating if the querent is single or has been feeling drained. In a current relationship, there may have been some stressors that indicate alone time for both would rejuvenate the relationship.

In a career or wealth reading, the four of swords suggests exhaustion and stress in the workplace or mental exhaustion around finances. It's time to take a break from those stresses and spend some time on anything that rejuvenates and catch up on rest.

If the card is pulled during a values and goals reading, prioritizing self-care and alone time when examining values and goals can help avoid burnout and stress.

5 OF SWORDS

5 OF SWORDS

Planet/sign: Aquarius

Decan: Venus

Corresponding dates: Roughly Jan. 21–Jan. 30

Element: Air

Numerology: 5: change

Colors: Blue, black, and gold

Symbols: Three figures, one picking up swords, two walking away toward water, and five clouds

Upright keywords: Walking away, surrender, emptiness after conflict, hostility, and stress

Reversed keywords: Reconciliation, clear communication, peaceful resolution, and compromise

Aquarius and the planet Venus both correspond with the five of swords card. Aquarius is an air sign that is related to the paradox between individuation and fitting in, whereas Venus represents relationships. The imagery suggests a drawing to an end after conflict rather than conflict itself. The nearest figure is picking up the swords as if to draw the conflict to a close. The figure closest to the water looks emotionally dejected as they near the water, moving away after the conflict. With Venus meaning relationships, this card is more about the damage that conflict brings to relationships than the conflict itself.

If the five of swords appears in a love and relationship reading, it indicates a stressful time during which conflict is brewing in a relationship. It is a warning that there are no winners in conflicts, so it might be better to pick up the pieces and find a way to reconcile or come to an agreement.

In a career or wealth reading, the five of swords suggests that there may be feelings of stress and intimidation in the workplace, whether real or an internal defensive response. Perhaps the leadership isn't strong or there's a lack of communication. This card can also mean financial disagreements. Take a step back and look at the bigger picture and find a way to reconcile.

Pulling the five of swords in a values and goals reading suggests that the querent should look at how they deal with conflict and conflict resolution, and set intentions to be more open to compromise.

6 OF SWORDS

6 OF SWORDS

Planet/sign: Aquarius

Decan: Mercury

Corresponding dates: Roughly Jan. 31–Feb. 9

Element: Air

Numerology: 6: harmony

Colors: Blue, white, and black

Symbols: Family in a boat rowing away, six swords facing down in boat, water, and land/town in distance

Upright keywords: Leaving past behind, releasing baggage, calm waters, and healing

Reversed keywords: Instability, stuck in the past, and not letting go

The six of swords is associated with the fixed sign of Aquarius and the Mercury decan, suggesting that this card is about gathering and collecting thoughts and releasing old mental patterns and baggage. Mercury represents the mind and communication. In Aquarius, Mercury represents the ability to see a way forward and to see the bigger picture, detaching from old ways of thinking. The six swords are pointing downward together in the card, signifying gathering thoughts within and reaching internal balance. The figures in the boat are moving toward stability in the form of the earth ahead, but they are moving through water, which brings emotional healing. The female and child figures are hooded with their heads bowed as if they are sad but still moving forward.

In a love and relationship reading, the six of swords indicates leaving stressful times behind. In an existing relationship, the family grouping in the boat suggests moving forward together rather than a separation. This can also mean leaving old family baggage and patterns behind.

If the six of swords appears in a career and wealth reading, it indicates that a calmer and more grounded period is arriving after a time of stress. This applies to either work or finances.

If the reading is about values and goals, the six of cups suggests a focus on leaving old problematic patterns behind and setting goals that are more aligned with what is desired and not with what has gone before.

7 OF SWORDS

7 OF SWORDS

Planet/sign: Aquarius

Decan: Moon

Corresponding dates: Roughly Feb. 10–Feb. 28/29, depending on the year

Element: Air

Numerology: 7: reflection

Colors: Black, white, and red

Symbols: Castle, male figure walking away carrying five swords, and two stuck in ground

Upright keywords: Deceit, risky behavior, sneakiness, stealth, and sabotage

Reversed keywords: Coming clean, regret, consequences, and truth revealed

Fixed sign Aquarius and the Moon decan correspond with the seven of swords card. Aquarius is a paradox of a sign—on one side of it is authoritarianism and on another is rebellion—sometimes making Aquarius the rebel without a cause. The Moon decan suggests that this card is connected to emotionally charged trouble of some kind. The card itself shows a man sneaking away from a castle and charging forward with one sword in one hand and four in the other hand together, while looking back toward the castle he's leaving. Two swords are left behind, suggesting that the figure is still connected to what is being left and that it's baggage. The card can point to deception of some kind or it can suggest not wanting to be a part of the consensus and trying to separate from that.

If the seven of swords appears in a love and relationship reading, it's a sign of caution if approaching new love interests, as things may not be as they first appear. It could also mean that the querent is not being entirely up front in a relationship. At its worst, someone could be pulling the wool over the other person's eyes and even being unfaithful.

In a career and wealth reading, the seven of swords indicates sabotage, gossip, or a scam around finances. It could also suggest that the querent is looking at get-rich-quick schemes or easy answers, when there is no easy way.

If the seven of swords appears in a goals and values reading, it represents a call to focus on living with integrity and awareness of others' motivations.

8 OF SWORDS

8 OF SWORDS

Planet/sign: Gemini

Decan: Jupiter

Corresponding dates: Roughly May 21–May 31

Element: Air

Numerology: 8: mastery

Colors: Gray, white, and gold

Symbols: Figure tied up and blindfolded, and eight swords stuck in the ground

Upright keywords: Feeling trapped, blindness, blocks, feeling powerless, and lack of vision

Reversed keywords: Release, freedom, vision, and escape

The sign of Gemini and the Jupiter decan correspond to the eight of swords card. Gemini is a mutable (change) sign that is about ideas, learning, curiosity, and adaptability. Jupiter is connected to the urge for freedom and something greater than ourselves. Like most of the swords cards, the upright reading of the image is that of restriction of vision, suggesting thoughts that limit the freedom and vision that is right in front of you. The blindfold, rope that ties, and ring of swords all lend this card the feeling of entrapment. However, there is an open space right in front of the figure, if only they could see it.

In a love and relationship reading, the eight of swords suggests an unwillingness or inability to stand up for yourself and to have strong boundaries in a relationship. It's also time to pull off the blinders of old ways of thinking so you can envision a brighter relationship future.

If the eight of swords appears in a career or wealth reading, it indicates that the querent may feel trapped in their role or in a financial situation and is unable to think beyond their current circumstances. It would be helpful to suggest keeping an open mind to new ideas so that perceptions can change.

In a goal and values reading, this card suggests that the querent may be very limited in their vision and that some brainstorming for possibilities could lead to a new sense of freedom.

9 OF SWORDS

9 OF SWORDS

Planet/sign: Gemini

Decan: Mars

Corresponding dates: Roughly June 1–June 11

Element: Air

Numerology: 9: accomplishment

Colors: Red, black, white, and green or blue

Symbols: Figure sitting up in bed with head in hands, swords on wall lying flat, and roses on the bedding

Upright keywords: Anxiety, nightmares, fears, worry, isolation, and overwhelm

Reversed keywords: Finding help, learning to cope, facing the shadow, and letting go

The nine of swords corresponds with Gemini and the Mars decan. Gemini is the energy of the mind, thoughts, and communication. Mars is the planet of passion, assertiveness, animal instincts, and anger. Mars in Gemini indicates cutting words and thoughts, and in this card, those thoughts are usually internalized. In the card, the figure is sitting up in bed with their head in their hands as if waking from a nightmare or unable to sleep because of fears and anxiety. The nine swords are hung flat on the wall, as if the thoughts are going nowhere. The sheets are red, which is the color of passion but also anger. And yet, the bed cover has roses on it, as if to say that self-care and love are in order to help process those fears, whether they are real or exaggerated in the mind.

If the nine of swords appears in a love and relationship reading, it likely points to anxiety and fears around a current relationship or regrets and sadness about past relationships. Something is haunting the mind, though this card is suggesting that the fears may be bigger than the actual thing the querent fears.

In a career and wealth reading, the nine of swords indicates a time of stress, worry, and even paranoia in the area or career or around finances. There's a big sense of overwhelm, which needs to be dealt with by looking at whether it's being caused by internal anxiety or external factors that can be changed.

If the reading is about values and goals, the nine of swords could be suggesting that the querent should get clear on what triggers overwhelm and stress to learn how to respond differently to those triggers in the future.

10 OF SWORDS

10 OF SWORDS

Planet/sign: Gemini

Decan: Sun

Corresponding dates: Roughly June 12–June 21

Element: Air

Numerology: 10: completion

Colors: Black, gray, blue, green, and gold

Symbols: Figure facedown on ground pierced by 10 swords, water behind, and rising full moon or Sun

Upright keywords: Endings, exhaustion, rock bottom, and hard times coming to an end

Reversed keywords: Rising above, recovery, survival, and lessons learned

The ten of swords is the last of the numbered cards in the suit and represents completion, but completion that may feel flat and defeated. However, the swords suit is related to the element of air and therefore represents what's going on in the mind. The sign of Gemini and the Sun decan correspond to this card, suggesting that new thoughts and ideas are on the horizon, especially with Gemini being a dual sign. This card is a reminder that changing your thoughts changes your life. This is completion, but not standing still. The figure depicted in the card, whose head is looking toward the water, suggests emotional healing. The full moon is a sign of completion and letting go. This could also be the Sun rising, as this is the Sun decan, offering a new beginning. It's time to let go of negative thought patterns and look toward a new beginning.

In a love and relationship reading, the ten of swords indicates a period of difficulty and possibly a relationship ending. There may be a sense of betrayal of some kind. If the querent can look beyond any hurt, they will see that healing is possible. It's a matter of perspective.

If the reading is about career and wealth, the ten of swords suggests cutting losses in situations that are bringing a feeling of exhaustion and mental overwhelm. The swords in the back suggest that the querent didn't see things coming but is being asked to look beyond to the healing elements behind the figure.

If the ten of swords appears in a reading focused on values and goals, this card suggests that the querent is being asked to work on limiting beliefs and thinking, because often it's our own thoughts and beliefs that keep us stuck.

THE PAGE OF SWORDS

PAGE OF SWORDS

Planet/sign: All air and earth signs—Gemini, Libra, Aquarius, Taurus, Virgo, and Capricorn

Decan: No decan

Corresponding dates: No dates

Element: Air/earth

Numerology: No number

Colors: Gold, white, green, and blue

Symbols: Walking figure dressed in gold and wielding a sword, clouds above, and mountains behind

Upright keywords: Inspiration, fairness, planning, curiosity, and mental agility

Reversed keywords: Lack of planning, scatterbrained, unfairness, gossip, and disappointing news

The Page of swords is the energy of earth and air and represents an inspired mental agility and fresh ideas. This card suggests that new and fresh ideas are coming, possibly from a messenger-type figure. The figure is standing on ground that is solid green, the color of innovation, and there are mountains behind them, suggesting that the ideas are promising. The figure is wielding the sword and is dressed in the color gold, suggesting that ideas and inspiration are bright. However, the solid ground is a call to stay grounded in the midst of enthusiasm.

In a love and relationship reading, the Page of swords can either indicate a relationship that exists on an intellectual level—more of a meeting of the minds rather than deep emotional connection initially. Explore this relationship with curiosity but also with some caution. Take it slow.

If the Page of swords appears in a career and wealth reading, it might suggest pursuing a career in an intellectual field or embarking on a new course of study for career advancement. There may also be new ideas for investments or ways to increase wealth.

In a values and goals reading, the Page of swords suggests that the querent is being asked to focus on increasing their knowledge base or on developing new ideas.

THE KNIGHT OF SWORDS

KNIGHT OF SWORDS

Planet/sign: All air signs—Gemini, Libra, and Aquarius

Decan: No decan

Corresponding dates: No dates

Element: Air

Numerology: No number

Colors: White, gray, and green

Symbols: Knight, holding sword aloft, a white horse, and trees

Upright keywords: Forward thinker, direct communication, honesty, sense of daring, and assertiveness

Reversed keywords: Lack of focus, lack of tact, vicious attitude, and arrogance

The Knight of swords corresponds to the element of air. Pure air moves quickly and has clarity of thought and communication. The Knight is charging forward and pointing his sword ahead. All the swords in tarot are double-edged, and this suggests that this form of daring, assertive communication and risk-taking isn't always welcomed by others. The querent may be overwhelmed by the quick thinking and ambitious energy of the person this card represents or may not be noticing any difficulties ahead.

In a love and relationship reading, the Knight of swords indicates a relationship with someone requiring a high level of intellectual stimulation. It can also point to the need to make some decisions in a relationship.

If the Knight of swords appears in a career and wealth reading, it's time to pursue your career and finance goals with focused intention. Be daring and take a few risks to achieve what's desired.

If the reading is about values and goals, the Knight of swords indicates a high level of clarity and the willingness to be assertive in the pursuit of goals.

THE QUEEN OF SWORDS

QUEEN OF SWORDS

Planet/sign: All water and air signs—Cancer, Scorpio, Pisces, Gemini, Libra, and Aquarius

Decan: No decan

Corresponding dates: No dates

Element: Air/water

Numerology: No number

Colors: Red, white, green, gray, and black

Symbols: Female figure in red holding a sword aloft, throne, butterflies, halos, trees, and clouds

Upright keywords: Independence, self-reliance, sharp mind, honesty, objectivity, and constructive criticism

Reversed keywords: Pessimism, critical attitude, cruelty, manipulation, and unforgiving nature

The Queen of swords is a mix of the air and water elements, which indicates that this is the epitome of emotional intelligence. She has a strong mind combined with compassion and love. The female figure on the card is sitting cross-legged, is relaxed, and is wearing red, the color of passion and love. The crown is slightly jaunty and the sword is held upright, suggesting sharpness of the mind. The throne is on solid ground, suggesting that this combination is powerful. The throne has butterflies, a symbol of transformation, while haloed heads looking outward in either direction suggest purity of intention.

If the Queen of swords appears in a love and relationship reading, the querent is likely being very discerning about a choice of partner or desiring a true partnership where there's a sense of independence. This can present as a new relationship with a person who needs space and has strong boundaries, or it could mean the querent needs this.

In a career and wealth reading, the Queen of swords suggests the presence of a person of high integrity and wisdom, perhaps a mentor who gives honest and constructive advice to help further the querent's career or financial growth. It can also indicate that the querent needs to use discernment to gain clarity in these areas.

If the reading is about values and goals, the Queen of swords suggests that a sense of fairness and a balance between the head and heart are present.

KING OF SWORDS

THE KING OF SWORDS

As a mix of air and fire, the King of Swords, is a balance between intellect and action, the mind and will, and, therefore, represents a person of high integrity that embodies responsibility through spiritual knowledge. This can mean a person in the querents life or the querent themselves and indicates a high level of integrity and clarity. The figure on the card sits in a very balanced, strong stance on the throne holding an upright sword, pointing to higher knowledge, with an open left hand in the receiving position. The golden crown symbolizes power and authority and the butterflies represent transformation. This indicates one who leads with high spiritual ethics.

In a love and relationship reading the King of Swords is not very romantic but has high standards and suggests a meeting of the minds rather than intense emotion. This makes for the kind of partnership that works towards ambitious goals together. This person will expect a lot from you but will also expect to be held to high standards.

If the King of Swords appears in a career and wealth reading this suggests high discipline and ethics. It could be a mentor that pushes you to hard to achieve your goals and may be somewhat strict and stern. This can also be the querent having high expectations of themselves.

If the reading is around values and goals the King of Swords is a suggestion to create clear and rigorous goals to aim for, based on very high values and ethics. Writing business plans or a list of resolutions is indicated.

Planet/sign: All air and fire signs—Gemini, Libra, Aquarius, Aries, Leo, and Sagittarius

Decan: No decan

Corresponding dates: No dates

Element: Air/fire

Numerology: No number

Colors: White and blue

Symbols: Figure on throne, upright sword, butterflies, crescent moons, and trees

Upright keywords: Rational thinking, authority, integrity, ethics, self-discipline, and strictness

Reversed keywords: Intimidation, cold, oppressiveness, and controlling behavior

10

THE MINOR ARCANA: WANDS

We next look at the suit of wands. Wands is the fire suit and associated with fire signs Aries, Leo, Sagittarius and fiery themes such as movement, action, creativity, life force, passion, will, assertiveness, and inspiration. The fire suit also corresponds to the first, fifth, and ninth houses.

THE ACE OF WANDS

ACE OF WANDS

Planet/sign: Aries, Leo, and Sagittarius

Decan: Aces are not associated with a decan

Corresponding dates: Aces are not given dates

Element: Fire

Numerology: 1: new beginnings

Colors: Blue, green, and gold

Symbols: Cloud/hand holding wand, light green land, water, and light brown mountains

Upright keywords: Exciting new beginnings, inspiration, new ideas, enthusiasm, and new initiative

Reversed keywords: Lack of direction, distraction, delays, and creative blocks

An understanding of the energies of the fire signs—Aries, Leo, and Sagittarius—and their rulers—Mars, the Sun, and Jupiter—can means that the ace of wands is associated with the fire of action, initiative, and creative inspiration. Fire moves fast and both burns things down and leaves space for new growth from the ashes. The sprouting wand on the card indicates the potential for new growth. The earth and mountains behind are lighter, fresher colors, also indicative of the new growth. The castle is grayed out as if to suggest that the old is being replaced by the new.

If the ace of wands is pulled in a love and relationship reading, it points to new or renewed excitement and passion in love. Relationship energy seems to provide a new lease on life; it is bold and ardent. This card can also suggest conception and a new life within this context.

In a career and wealth reading, the ace of wands indicates new beginnings and/or excitement and passion in these areas. It heralds a time of positivity and potential and a period of growth. However, it comes with a slight caution against taking reckless financial risks, as fire tends to be rash.

If goals and values are the focus of the reading, this card suggests guiding the querent to create goals based on passionate and inspired values. This is a time to shoot for the stars.

2 OF WANDS

2 OF WANDS

Planet/sign: Aries

Decan: Mars

Corresponding dates: Roughly March 21–March 30

Element: Fire

Numerology: 2: balance

Colors: Green, blue, and brown

Symbols: Figure standing on castle, one wand in hand, other planted by figure, orb/globe, water, and mountains

Upright keywords: Planning, exploring options, decisions, holding the world in hands, and new phase/goals

Reversed keywords: Lack of planning, fear of moving forward, and playing it safe

Mars is the planet of action, drive, and life force and is the ruler of the sign Aries. This card is about finding balance between the excitement of new beginnings and the planning and decisions required to create goals and bring desires to fruition.

If this card appears in a query about love and relationships, it could indicate that there's an imbalance between two people and that equilibrium needs to be restored. It could also be a message to balance love/work life or that the querent is juggling responsibilities.

In a career and wealth reading, this card indicates that a level of stability has been attained and that it's a good time to explore long-term options and plans in either or both areas.

If the two of wands appears in a reading about goals and values, it suggests that there is great clarity around values and that it's time to set aspirational goals for the future.

3 OF WANDS

3 OF WANDS

Planet/sign: Aries

Decan: Sun

Corresponding dates: Roughly March 31–April 10

Element: Fire

Numerology: 3: creation

Colors: Black, blue, light brown, and sand

Symbols: Standing figure facing the distance, three wands planted in ground, figure holding one, sailboat, and mountains

Upright keywords: Expansion, looking ahead, progress, thinking outside the box, and momentum

Reversed keywords: Inability to see way forward, delays, obstacles, and limitations

The Sun is the core self or innate character, and Aries is the pioneer, the initiator, or leader who is very sure of themselves. The three of wands therefore suggests someone who is very solid and secure and ready to forge ahead with new projects and creations. The three wands planted in the ground indicate a solid basis on which to build, as if success has been achieved with current endeavors. The mountains in the distance and the sailboat indicate moving toward greater ambitions and expansion. The figure is looking ahead to new horizons while surrounded by the solidity of their prior endeavors.

In a love and relationship reading, the three of wands suggests a strong future for either an established relationship or a new relationship. This card indicates looking to and creating the future together.

If the reading is about career and wealth, the three of wands indicates a strong period of growth and creativity in these areas. This could mean a new job, business or investment opportunity or expansion overseas.

If the card is pulled in a goals and values reading, it suggests that the goals can be built upon what has already been achieved. This is a time to expand horizons.

4 OF WANDS

4 OF WANDS

The four of wands corresponds with Venus and Aries. Venus is the planet of love, beauty, harmony, and manifestation, whereas Aries is the sign of life force and will. The four of wands therefore represents a time of energized fulfilment and abundance, perhaps a celebration of life with the community or family for overall wealth and love. This is a time to pause and show gratitude for everything—love, abundance, and the home—and to allow yourself the feeling of satisfaction.

In a love and relationship reading, the four of wands represents either a celebration of a life created together or the start of a new life in partnership. This is a celebration that spills out into the community, so it could suggest a wedding or anniversary.

If the reading is about career and wealth, the four of wands suggests a pinnacle of stability and a sharing of that feeling of abundance. This could mean a celebration with work colleagues or giving of gifts to share abundance with others.

If this is a goals and values reading, the card indicates an attitude of gratitude and celebration for a life well lived so far. It suggests setting new goals to maintain that stability and feeling of fulfilment.

Planet/sign: Aries

Decan: Venus

Corresponding dates: Roughly April 11–April 20

Element: Fire

Numerology: 4: foundation

Colors: Green, purple, and black

Symbols: Two figures dancing barefoot, four wands growing grapes, and a castle

Upright keywords: Abundance, belonging, community, celebrations, and joy

Reversed keywords: Lack of roots, conflict with others, and lack of support

5 OF WANDS

5 OF WANDS

Planet/sign: Leo

Decan: Saturn

Corresponding dates: Roughly July 21–July 31

Element: Fire

Numerology: 5: change

Colors: Gold, white, green, and black

Symbols: Five figures in conflict with wands as weapons

Upright keywords: Conflict, competition, chaos, disagreements, and diversity

Reversed keywords: Cooperation, agreements, and truce

The five of wands corresponds with Saturn, the planet of limitation, boundaries, mastery, and patience; and Leo is the sign of courage, joy, and enthusiasm, but also of the ego and sovereignty. This card suggests a conflict and butting of heads, as Saturn tries to lay down the law and Leo likes to be the leader and doesn't enjoy their bubble of enthusiasm being burst. The card itself shows five figures in conflict with each other and crossing their wands or blocking them.

In a love and relationship reading, the five of wands could indicate a warning that playful disagreements could turn into conflict if either partner, or both, becomes overly authoritarian and forceful. If looking for love, there's a caution against being too strong and forceful, as that might push potential partners away.

If the five of wands comes up in a reading about career and wealth, there may be an air of competition or conflict in the workplace. This can point to an industry that is naturally competitive, so it's not necessarily a bad thing for everyone. There is a clash of egos and some financial instability.

If the reading is about goals and values, the five of wands suggests internal conflict, stress, and a lack of clear direction. Potentially, this stress might be around limiting beliefs—thinking that things should be a certain way rather than tuning in to the heart to find what is really desired.

6 OF WANDS

6 OF WANDS

Planet/sign: Leo

Decan: Jupiter

Corresponding dates: Roughly Aug. 1–Aug. 10

Element: Fire

Numerology: 6: harmony

Colors: Green, gold, white, and gray

Symbols: Figure riding light gray or white horse, victory wreaths, and other figures holding wands in celebration

Upright keywords: Success, confidence, recognition, praise, and victory

Reversed keywords: Failure, lack of confidence, egoism, and lack of recognition

Jupiter is the planet of abundance, luck, and expansion, and Leo is the sign that loves to shine and lead. These correspond with the six of wands. Jupiter and Leo combined shine like a big, red balloon, loving accolades and feeling very self-confident and successful. However, this energy also needs praise and recognition. This card brings the energy of success and recognition and is a sign of receiving a level of fulfilment and pride for achievements.

If the six of wands appears in a love and relationship reading, it suggests a high level of happiness and fulfilment in these areas. Leo rules the heart, and the six of wands says that the heart is full and prospects for continued happiness are high.

In a reading about career and wealth, this card corresponds with a pinnacle of success and recognition and suggests reaping the rewards after a period of hard work and investment.

If the card appears in a goals and values reading, it suggests that the querent get clear on their heart's desires to set audacious and ambitious goals. Now is not a time for limiting potential.

7 OF WANDS

7 OF WANDS

Planet/sign: Leo

Decan: Mars

Corresponding dates: Roughly Aug. 11–Aug. 20

Element: Fire

Numerology: 7: reflection

Colors: Purple, gold, and brown

Symbols: Figure holding one wand with six wands pointed at the figure

Upright keywords: Strong will, patience, taking a stand for the self, determination, and a defending position

Reversed keywords: Giving up, quitting, lack of belief in self, and surrendering

The seven of wands corresponds to the Mars decan of Leo and indicates protecting the self or maintaining levels of achievements. This is the last of the fixed sign cards (five through seven) before cards that bring forward movement. Mars is our protector or guardian and stands ready to fight off any attempts to hurt. Leo is our ego, our heart-led self, that can also be very fragile and easily hurt or toppled from the throne of confidence. In this card, the figure is holding one wand against six others and is looking at the wand for protective strength. The figure is in gold and the background is purple—both colors of royalty and wealth—suggesting that the querent is defending their position and achievements.

If the seven of wands is pulled in a love and relationship reading, it suggests that some strong boundaries are being called for in relationships. A relationship may even have to defend itself against outside forces. It's not a time to let others, or the partner, have control over the querent.

In a career and wealth reading, the seven of wands indicates that the querent's position at work may be under some sort of threat, or that they feel threatened in some way. The card is saying that the person must stay strong and that they have what it takes to maintain their achievements.

If the seven of wands appears in a values and goals reading, this is a call to work on developing confidence in the self by looking at strengths and building on those.

8 OF WANDS

8 OF WANDS

The eight of wands corresponds with the first of the mutable numbered cards and the mutable fire sign, Sagittarius. The eight corresponds with the Mercury decan of Sagittarius. Mercury represents the mind, communication, and ideas, whereas Sagittarius is the sign associated with swiftness, forward movement, freedom, and inspiration. In the card, the eight wands are suspended in the air and flying through a sparkling, dawn-colored background. The wands are aimed at water as if to integrate the energy of fire (inspiration) and air (thought) with feelings and emotion. There are no figures in this card—it's pure inspiration and forward movement of thought and ideas. After the difficulties of the previous card, the eight suggests strong momentum to move away from difficulties.

In a love and relationship reading, the eight of wands means that excitement is on the horizon, possibly after a time of conflict and feeling stuck. There may be a new relationship on the horizon or a renewal of excitement in a current partnership.

If the eight of wands appears in a career and wealth reading, it is indicating rapid growth in career and wealth. The mind is bursting with inspiration and ideas, though there may be a tendency to act rashly in money matters.

In a goals and values reading, this card invites the querent to think about the future and what ideas and inspiration are informing where they want to aim for. They may have been lacking inspiration and excitement, so they will need to find what gets them fired up.

Planet/sign: Sagittarius

Decan: Mercury

Corresponding dates: Roughly Nov. 21–Nov. 30

Element: Fire

Numerology: 8: mastery

Colors: Blue, yellow, brown, and green

Symbols: Eight wands flying over and toward water and a clear sparkling background

Upright keywords: Momentum, fast movement, progress, and excitement

Reversed keywords: Losing momentum, missed opportunities, and delays

9 OF WANDS

9 OF WANDS

Planet/sign: Sagittarius

Decan: Moon

Corresponding dates: Roughly Dec. 1–Dec. 10

Element: Fire

Numerology: 9: accomplishment

Colors: Purple, green, and brown

Symbols: Figure in purple holding a wand with bandage around head, eight wands planted firmly in ground behind figure, and a triangular pendant

Upright keywords: Persistence, determination, resilience, and battle weariness

Reversed keywords: Defensiveness, pointless struggle, uncompromising attitude, stubbornness

The nine of wands corresponds with the sign of Sagittarius and the Moon decan. Sagittarius is the sign of exploration, new experiences, questing, and aspiration; and the Moon represents emotional receptivity, feelings, and security. In this card, the figure stands firm but appears to be wounded, as shown by the bandage around the head. The triangular pendant on the chest suggests integrating the mind, body, and spirit to heal and move forward. The eight firmly planted wands behind the figure suggest strength and mastery gained from previous trials in life, and the one wand suggests a new beginning. The card means that resilience and strength can be gained from difficult times and that it's time to move forward for a new start with determination.

If the nine of wands appears in a love and relationship reading, it indicates that the querent gets to work through old relationship issues and traumas so that they heal and move forward in a new way. Relationships can be successful if both partners are prepared to heal old wounds.

In a career and wealth reading, the nine of wands tells us that work life and finances may be under some pressure, but that this feeling of strife can be overcome with persistence. New starts are coming.

In a goals and values reading, the card is a call to get clear on emotional needs and security so that future goals can be created that address those needs. These needs may not have been addressed until now.

10 OF WANDS

10 OF WANDS

The ten of wands is the last of the numbered cards in the wands suit and corresponds with completion. As a Sagittarius card in the Saturn decan, the restrictive nature of Saturn dampens the enthusiasm and fire of Sagittarius. Saturn is indicative of limitations, hard work, and a heavy load, and that's the energy of this card. Sagittarius is inspiration, fast-moving energy, and fire. After the journey through the wands, this card indicates burnout and a feeling of heaviness rather than excitement, illustrated by the figure carrying the heavy load of the 10 wands—a symbol of completion—but seemingly unable to see the fruits of this time, as the trees and buildings in the background suggest.

If the ten of wands appears in a love and relationship reading, it indicates that love life and relationships are not feeling the spark of excitement, whether that's because outer responsibilities are weighing the querent down or they are experiencing a general feeling of loneliness and heaviness. It's important to express this to a partner at this time so they don't feel shut out.

In career and wealth matters, this card points to overwork, too many responsibilities, too many projects, or projects that are too large. It can also indicate that debts and expenses are a heavy load and that the querent may not be able to see a way to manage all these burdens. It's a time to ask for help.

In a values and goals context, the ten of wands suggests taking an inventory of responsibilities or an inability to ask for help and to receive it. Set goals to ask for and to receive help, and to let go of the tendency to do everything alone.

Planet/sign: Sagittarius

Decan: Saturn

Corresponding dates: Roughly Dec. 11–Dec. 21

Element: Fire

Numerology: 10: completion

Colors: Green, gold, black, and white

Symbols: Male figure, dejected, carrying 10 wands, separated from connection/home

Upright keywords: Heavy load, responsibility, burden, challenges, and lost focus

Reversed keywords: Lack of stamina, overworking, and feeling worn out with too much responsibility

THE PAGE OF WANDS

PAGE OF WANDS

Planet/sign: All fire and earth signs—Aries, Leo, Sagittarius, Taurus, Virgo, and Capricorn

Decan: No decan

Corresponding dates: No dates

Element: Earth/fire

Numerology: No number

Colors: White, green, and light brown

Symbols: Young figure focused on and carrying wand, mountains, and looking to the future

Upright keywords: Optimism, fresh ideas, creative spark, and adventure

Reversed keywords: Impatience, lack of motivation, lack of inspiration, and immaturity

The court cards correspond to the elements rather than any one sign, planetary body, decan, or a date range, and usually represent a person or the querent themselves. The Page of wands corresponds with the earth and fire elements, according to the Order of the Golden Dawn. Therefore, it points to a major focus on grounded inspiration and fresh, creative possibilities and inspiration. The earth element is about manifestation in the physical world, and fire is the energy of the creative spark. The mountains in the background suggest big possibilities in these fresh ideas, but this is in the idea stage only right now.

In a love and relationship reading the Page of wands can suggest new and exciting love interests or renewed excitement in a current relationship. This usually indicates relationships that involve new experiences and adventures.

If the Page of wands appears in a career and wealth reading, this card indicates new excitement and possibilities for achievement and creation in both areas. This is in the idea stage, an eagerness for new horizons, rather than the active pursuant of those ideas.

In a values and goals reading, the Page of wands indicates clarity around values in relation to creativity and willingness to explore. It suggests setting aside time for new adventures and experience.

THE KNIGHT OF WANDS

KNIGHT OF WANDS

Planet/sign: Fire and air signs—Aries, Leo, Sagittarius, Gemini, Libra, and Aquarius

Decan: No decan

Corresponding dates: No dates

Element: Fire/air

Numerology: No number

Colors: Gold, gray, brown, and green

Symbols: Armored figure riding gold horse, wand held up and forward, horse rearing in excitement, and salamanders

Upright keywords: Adventure, new experiences, taking risks, courage, and free spirit

Reversed keywords: Recklessness, showing off, lack of self-control, and volatility

The Knight of wands goes with the elements of air and fire, which indicates fast-moving, volatile energy, as air fans the flames of fire. The Knight is moving forward on the rearing horse, a symbol of strength, motion, and vitality, but it looks as if air is making the fiery horse difficult to control. The wand is being held forward at arm's length and upright as if to allow the air to push it forward. The salamanders on the Knight's cloak symbolize the transformative energy of this card. The card in this deck is almost all gold, a color of creativity and inspiration.

If the Knight of wands is drawn in a love and relationship reading, it can indicate a person who is exciting and fearless but also volatile and impulsive, so they may not be the right one for a long-term relationship. In a long-term relationship, this card can also suggest a period of excitement and adventure that can also be unsettling.

In a career and wealth reading, the Knight of wands corresponds with passion, excitement, and new projects that may be both exciting and a little scary. There's an eagerness for new roles, projects, or even a new path. In finance terms, unexpected money may be coming in, but there may also be a tendency for unadvisable risk-taking.

If the Knight of wands appears in a reading about values and goals, the card suggests that the querent has been lacking inspiration and adventure in their life and must examine their values around new experiences and set goals accordingly.

THE QUEEN OF WANDS

QUEEN OF WANDS

Planet/sign: Water and fire signs—Cancer, Scorpio, Pisces, Aries, Leo, and Sagittarius

Decan: No decan

Corresponding dates: No dates

Element: Fire/water

Numerology: No number

Colors: Gold, green, brown, and black

Symbols: Crowned regal female figure dressed in gold, lions, black cat, and flowers

Upright keywords: Courage, creativity, assertiveness, bringer of new life, magic, and confidence

Reversed keywords: Lacking confidence, selfish, demanding, and temperamental attitude

The elements of water and fire correspond with the Queen of wands, and water tends to temper the rashness of fire and bring in emotional strength to the mix. This is the energy of confidence that comes from strength, both emotionally and creatively. The Queen sits on a green (nature) throne looking intently forward to the future, dressed in the creative and abundant color of gold. A black cat, a symbol of magic, appears at her feet, and she is surrounded by lions (strength) and flowers (new growth). This is the embodiment of wise courage and creativity.

In a love and relationship reading, the Queen of wands points to a self-assured and magical relationship or person. This could indicate a couple starting out on a new and promising healthy relationship, or a growing sense of confidence, intimacy, and spark in a current relationship.

If the Queen of wands is pulled in a career and wealth reading, it is a wonderful omen and indicates great confidence, energy, and bravery to take on new work-related goals and projects. It can also suggest an inspirational mentor or leader that helps the querent in their work and/or financial life.

In a values and goals reading, the Queen of wands may indicate a time when values around a person's self-confidence and willingness to grow are at the forefront. It's time for courageous goals.

THE KING OF WANDS

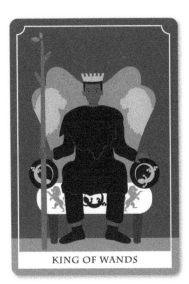

KING OF WANDS

The last of the suit of wands is the King. Bringing charisma, leadership, motivation, and optimism, fire signs tend to have natural leadership qualities and can inspire others into action. In the Tarot, the King of wands is dressed in black and sits on the throne looking directly at the person looking at the card, holding the wand in one hand, indicating authority. The King is surrounded by symbols of fire and leadership, like the lion, and transformation, like the salamander. The green is a color of abundance.

If the King of wands appears in a love and relationship reading, this indicates an exciting, charismatic, and energetic partner. This is a good card in a love reading, as it points to passion and depth. However, this much fire can also be draining for some, and there may be some fiery spats.

In a career and wealth reading, the King of wands indicates success, leadership, and stability. The querent is likely to be in a very stable financial position. In career, they are likely to be in a position of mentorship.

If the reading is about values and goals, it's time to aim for leadership and success. What does success mean for this individual? This card calls for getting clear on that question and setting goals according to those answers.

Planet/sign: Fire signs—Aries, Leo, and Sagittarius

Decan: No decan

Corresponding dates: No dates

Element: Fire

Numerology: No number

Colors: Green, gold, black, and white

Symbols: Crowned male figure, wand, throne, lions, and salamanders

Upright keywords: Strength, motivation, protectiveness, bold action, leadership, and optimism

Reversed keywords: Ineffective leader, domineering character, rudeness, and passiveness

A FINAL WORD

Congratulations on making it through the book. However, this is not a book to be read once and put away. This is a reference to be used alongside your actual cards. Keep studying the cards and the astrological elements in the cards and using this book as a tool until your understanding grows and this information starts to become second nature. Use the suggested keywords for planets, signs, and houses, but also find your own. Find keywords for the numbered cards that work for you.

You might choose to use a different deck, or decks, than the one portrayed throughout this book. There are common themes that run through all tarot decks, and the astrological symbolism is reflected in all decks, so a basic understanding of the astrology will help you with every tarot deck.

Play with spreads, look at how the cards work with each other, get to know the elements, think of synonyms for the few keywords in this book, and look at how the colors work with the astrology.

Keep a notebook and/or use this book's accompanying workbook and the deck referenced to write down your thoughts and insights.

Primarily, have patience and start where you are. Both astrology and tarot are endless, magical rabbit holes, and knowledge and understanding deepen over time. I still learn new things daily after more than 30 years of study.

I will leave you with words I used several times at the beginning of the book and throughout. Practice, practice, practice. But also, there is never a point where this journey ends, so begin where you are.

SUN TABLE

SIGN	SYMBOL	APPROX. DATES	RULING PLANETS	ENERGY
ARIES	♈	March 21–April 20	Mars	Day/Inhale
TAURUS	♉	Apr. 21–May 20	Venus	Night/Exhale
GEMINI	♊	May 21–June 20	Mercury	Day/Inhale
CANCER	♋	June 21–July 20	Moon	Night/Exhale
LEO	♌	July 21–Aug. 20	Sun	Day/Inhale
VIRGO	♍	Aug. 21–Sept. 20	Mercury	Night/Exhale
LIBRA	♎	Sept. 21–Oct. 20	Venus	Day/Inhale
SCORPIO	♏	Oct. 21–Nov. 20	Mars - Traditional Pluto - Modern	Night/Exhale
SAGITTARIUS	♐	Nov. 21–Dec. 20	Jupiter	Day/Inhale
CAPRICORN	♑	Dec. 21–Jan. 20	Saturn	Night/Exhale
AQUARIUS	♒	Jan. 21–Feb. 20	Saturn - Traditional Uranus - Modern	Day/Inhale
PISCES	♓	Feb. 21–Mar. 20	Jupiter - Traditional Neptune - Modern	Night/Exhale

GLOSSARY

12 HOUSES: The houses are numbered one through twelve, moving counterclockwise. Houses represent areas of life, such as the seventh house, which represents significant relationships.

AIR SIGNS: Gemini, Libra, and Aquarius, which are related to the mind and communication.

ANGULAR HOUSES: The first in each quadrant of the chart, the first, fourth, seventh, and tenth houses.

ASPECT: An angular relationship between two planetary bodies or chart points.

ASTROLOGY: The study of the movement and cycles of the planetary bodies in the universe and how those influences work in human lives and in the natural world.

CADENT: The second in each quadrant of the chart, the second, fifth, eighth, and eleventh houses.

CARDINAL MODALITY: Aries, Cancer, Libra, and Capricorn, known as initiating signs.

COURT CARDS: The four court cards in each suit are the Page, Knight, Queen, and King. They are also known as trumps.

CUSP: The transition point between two signs or houses.

DECAN: A 10-degree division of the zodiac. There are three decans for each sign.

DIVINATION: From the Latin *divinus*, meaning to be inspired by the divine, this is the practice of seeking divine knowledge or messages.

EARTH SIGNS: Taurus, Virgo, and Capricorn, which are related to material and earthly matters.

FIRE SIGNS: Aries, Leo, and Sagittarius, which are related to transformation, inspiration, and action.

FIXED MODALITY: Taurus, Leo, Scorpio, and Aquarius, which relate to love, stability, and making things that last.

LUMINARIES: The Sun and Moon, also referred to as the lights.

MAJOR ARCANA: The 22 trump cards revealing secrets and mysteries (Arcana) and major life events.

MINOR ARCANA: The four suits, consisting of 56 cards with 14 cards in each suit. There are 10 numbered and four court cards, which relate to mundane events.

MODALITIES (QUADRUPLICITIES): Cardinal (initiating), fixed (solidifying), and mutable (change). There are four astrological signs in each modality.

MUTABLE MODALITY: Gemini, Virgo, Sagittarius, and Pisces, which are changeable signs.

NATAL: Characteristics and life path based on date, time, and location of birth.

NUMEROLOGY: The study of the significance and meaning of numbers.

PERSONAL PLANETS: Visible planets representing basic human drives—Mercury, Venus, and Mars. Jupiter and Saturn are social planets sometimes referred to as personal or transpersonal planets.

PLANETARY CYCLES (ORBITAL PERIODS): The length of time taken for a planetary body to orbit another object.

QUERENT: The person asking for guidance from the Tarot.

RIDER-WAITE TAROT DECK: One of first major and most widely popular decks created by mystic A. E. Waite, illustrated by Pamela Coleman Smith, and published by Rider, now often known as the Rider-Waite-Smith Deck or the Waite-Smith Deck.

SIGNIFICATOR: A card representing the querent, or person seeking guidance.

SUCCEDENT: The third and final house in each quadrant of the chart, the third, sixth, ninth, and twelfth.

SUIT OF CUPS: The suit representing the element of water and emotional issues.

SUIT OF PENTACLES: The suit representing the element of earth and material issues.

SUIT OF SWORDS: The suit representing the element of air and issues of the mind.

SUIT OF WANDS: The suit representing the element of fire and creativity and spirituality.

SUN SIGNS: The 12 signs into which the zodiac is divided, reflecting the Sun's apparent movement from Earth.

THOTH DECK: A widely used and popular tarot deck created by Aleister Crowley with art by Frieda Harris.

TRANSIT: The ongoing movement of the planets.

TRANSPERSONAL PLANETS: The planets orbiting beyond Saturn and representing larger social cycles—Uranus, Neptune, and Pluto.

TRIPLICITIES: A group of three signs belonging to the same element.

WATER SIGNS: Cancer, Scorpio, and Pisces, which are related to emotions and intuition.

RESOURCES

APPS

Golden Thread Tarot
Readings and lessons

Labyrinthos
Free readings and courses

Trusted Tarot
Free and paid options for readings

ASTROLOGY WEBSITES

Astro.CafeAstrology.com/natal.php
Create a free natal chart online.

Astro.com/horoscope
Create a free natal chart online.

CafeAstrology.com
A fabulous reference site for all things related to astrology.

BOOKS

Arienn, Angeles. *The Tarot Handbook: Practical Applications of Ancient Visual Symbols.* New York: Jeremy P. Tarcher/Putnam; 1st edition, 1997.

Edington, Louise. *The Complete Guide to Astrology: Understanding Yourself, Your Signs, and Your Birth Chart.* Emeryville, CA: Rockridge Press, 2021.

Edington, Louise. *Modern Astrology: Harness the Stars to Discover Your Soul's True Purpose.* Emeryville, CA: Althea Press, 2018.

Forrest, Steven. *The Inner Sky: How to Make Wiser Choices for a More Fulfilling Life.* Borrego Springs, CA: Seven Paws Press; Reprint edition, 2012.

Pollack, Rachel. *Seventy-Eight Degrees of Wisdom: A Tarot Journey to Self-Awareness.* Newburyport, MA: Weiser Books, 2020.

Reed, Theresa. *Tarot: No Questions Asked: Mastering the Art of Intuitive Reading.* Newburyport, MA: Weiser Books, 2020.

Wen, Benebell. *Holistic Tarot: An Integrative Approach to Using Tarot for Personal Growth.* Berkeley, CA: North Atlantic Books, 2015.

RECOMMENDED TAROT DECKS FOR BEGINNERS

Rider-Waite-Smith Tarot Deck

This is the most popular and widely used of the tarot decks. The well-known imagery and symbolism of Rider-Waite-Smith cards have inspired the creation of other decks and are ideal for beginners learning to read tarot.

Light Seer's Tarot Deck

This deck translates the meanings of the cards by using contemporary and intuitive characters in the images. The cards are expressive, magical, and full of tarot symbolism.

Modern Witch Tarot Deck

Diverse people and modern situations are presented in this updated Rider-Waite-Smith–style deck. The cards are youthful and vibrant while still holding traditional relevance in their meanings.

Superlunaris Tarot Deck

Inspiring and interesting characters make up this reworked deck that embraces modern themes. The people portrayed on these vivid and empowering cards are relatable and engaging.

TAROT WEBSITES

BiddyTarot.com
Labyrinthos.co
Tarot.com

TheTarotGuide.com
TarotfortheWildSoul.com

REFERENCES

Arienn, Angeles. *The Tarot Handbook: Practical Applications of Ancient Visual Symbols.* New York: Jeremy P. Tarcher/Putnam; 1st edition, 1997.

Edington, Louise. *The Complete Guide to Astrology: Understanding Yourself, Your Signs, and Your Birth Chart.* Emeryville, CA: Rockridge Press, 2021.

Edington, Louise. *Modern Astrology: Harness the Stars to Discover Your Soul's True Purpose.* Emeryville, CA: Althea Press, 2018.

Forrest, Steven. *The Inner Sky: How to Make Wiser Choices for a More Fulfilling Life.* Borrego Springs, CA: Seven Paws Press; Reprint edition, 2012.

Pollack, Rachel. *Seventy-Eight Degrees of Wisdom: A Tarot Journey to Self-Awareness.* Newburyport, MA: Weiser Books, 2020.

INDEX

ABOUT THE AUTHOR

 **Louise Edington** has been studying and practicing astrology as an interest for more than 30 years and has been working professionally as an evolutionary astrologer since 2012. Known as the Cosmic Owl of Cosmic Owl Astrology, Louise loves to combine all her passions as an astrologer, writer, shamanic healer, and certified hypnotherapy and past life regression therapist.

Louise helps clients regain a deep connection with the cycles of the universe so that they create an extraordinary life experience. She provides astrological counseling, astrology classes, and a membership community.

You may learn more about her services at LouiseEdington.com.

Louise's books *The Complete Guide to Astrology* and *Modern Astrology: Harness the Stars to Discover Your Soul's True Purpose* are available at all major bookstores, including indie outlets.